Slaves of Slaves

The Challenge of Latin American Women

Latin American and Caribbean Women's Collective

Translated by Michael Pallis

82- 948

Zed Press, 57 Caledonian Road, London N1 9DN.

Slaves of Slaves was first published by *des femmes*, 2 rue de la Roquette, 75011 Paris under the title *Mujeres*. First published in English by Zed Press, 57 Caledonian Road, London N1 9DN in October 1980.

ISBN Hb 0 86232 006 2
      Pb 0 86232 001 1

Typed by Gill Bussell
Designed by Mayblin/Shaw
Copyedited by Beverley Brown
Typeset by Jenny Duley
Proofread by Sue Stark and Hilary Arnot
Cover design by Jacque Solomons
Printed by Redwood Burn Ltd., Trowbridge and Esher
Cover photo courtesy of Contemporary Archives on Latin America

U.S. Distributor:
Lawrence Hill and Co., 520 Riverside Avenue, Westport, Conn. 06880, U.S.A.

Contents

Preface

This book is written out of a belief that the only way to understand the problems of Latin American and Caribbean women is through an investigation specifically geared to the complex and contradictory world they live in. Over the last few years, a general awareness of the 'problem of women' has developed, due largely to the influence of feminist movements in the industrialized world. Women's issues are now very much on the agenda.

Since 1974 information campaigns and propaganda, sometimes even publicity in the mass media, have reached millions of people. 1975 was declared 'International Women's Year'. The United Nations World Conference in Mexico led to a variety of legal reforms aimed at 'advancing the position of women', as well as to a wide range of publications on the same theme. In the meantime, a great many women's groups have been set up or have consolidated themselves; unfortunately a number of these have become increasingly distanced from the struggles and day-to-day realities experienced by most Latin American women.

Aware of the danger of mechanically transposing foreign models to other contexts, we felt that it was essential to define the particular character and meaning of a women's movement in Latin America. In an attempt to confront the 'question of women' as we have encountered it in practice, we formed a group of Latin American women which has met regularly in Paris since 1972. Today, after many changes and transformations, and thanks to the contributions of women from the Caribbean, we can finally present the outcome of our inquiries along with various documents and accounts of the condition of women in our continent. The multiplicity and diversity of day-to-day realities in the various regions of Latin America and the Caribbean does not mean that one cannot detect patterns which allow one to draw up an overall analysis of women's situation there.

Generally, when one speaks of Latin America, one means the American continent from the Rio Grande in Mexico to Tierra del Fuego in Patagonia, as well as the Antilles. Cuba, Puerto Rico, Haiti and the Dominican Republic, Guadeloupe, Martinique, Jamaica, Trinidad and Tobago, Barbados, etc. are usually excluded, despite the fact that these islands are far closer to Latin America than to their 'metropoles' (France, Britain, the U.S., and Holland). It is true that Spanish or Portuguese are not the main languages on the islands. Like the rest of the Latin American continent, they have belonged to several different European colonial empires. They have been used as strategic points from which to develop and maintain colonial domination, whether as sources of raw materials for the metropoles or as outposts for the slave trade and other commerce. In these islands more than anywhere else, conquest and colonization has meant the extermination of the indigenous populations and the substitution of other ethnic groups forcibly imported from parts of Africa as labourers for the *conquistadores*. Furthermore, isolationist policies of the rival colonial empires in the area naturally prevented either the growth of solidarity between these countries or their autonomous development.

Today, with the exception of Cuba, the old structures are practically unchanged, despite more than a century of 'independence' for Latin America and most of the islands. Some of them still have special status, as in the case of Guadeloupe and Martinique which are French overseas '*Departements*', or Puerto Rico, a 'Free Associated State' of the United States. Despite this specific historical context, we are now at a stage when the islands and the continent as a whole face analogous realities and and common problems. One of these is the situation of women, which is why we are seeking to do away with colonialism's artificial dividing line and to use a perspective which takes in both the Antilles and Latin America proper.

Problems such as endemic unemployment, grossly inadequate sanitation, lack of educational facilities and sometimes even generalized illiteracy exist in different degrees throughout Latin America. These differences are characteristics of each particular social formation and the unequal development of their productive forces. Naturally all these problems have direct consequences for the condition of women. But this condition is made far worse by the colonial inheritance, the influence of religion, specific cultural traditions, *machismo* and the social values which derive from it, not to mention the economic and cultural domination which has long been the lot of the Latin American people as a whole.

Before we go on, a few points about how the work that has gone into this book has been organized—we chose to work collectively, and, despite all the difficulties we encountered as a result, this enabled us to advance a common analysis as well as stimulating our individual creativity. Also, an inter-disciplinary approach seemed essential if we were to present a comprehensive picture of such a complex problematic. Another reason was that we wanted to encourage everybody who participated in the group to write, in order to overcome the timidity, insecurity and fear which not writing may induce, especially as, even today, women are generally cut off from the experience of writing.

Nonetheless some of the women who worked with us did not participate in actually drawing up this text, in some cases because they had already returned to their country of origin. However, their contribution helped us to become more fully aware of the problem of women and made our initial approach much more precise. All the articles are the result of collective effort. One or several of the participants would prepare a draft which was then discussed, corrected and added to by the group as a whole. Although most of us are Spanish-speaking, we wanted to present our work in French as well as Spanish. We are grateful to those who helped us by reading and correcting the original manuscript.

The participants themselves come from a wide range of backgrounds. Often, professional and personal factors have determined the scope of the work we could undertake. As we did not have women from every part of the continent in the group we could not cover each individual country. But out aim was not in any case to present an exhaustive study. On the contrary, we sought only to approach the problem from our own perspectives, in the hope that the result might help others to a better understanding of the issues facing Latin American women. Thanks to *Les editions des femmes*, this meeting and exchange of experiences by women from different Latin American countries has found concrete expression.

The book is divided into two Parts. In the First Part we attempt to draw out some general ideas on the specificity of the women's movement in Latin America and the Caribbean, taking into account both the particularities and the similarities specific to the area. Then we present a historical summary of the struggles and movements organized by women. We conclude the section with an attempt to show the dangers of arbitrarily transplanting to Latin America goals proper to the struggle of women's movements in the developed countries, and take as an example of this the 'wages for housework' campaign, which we in fact see as a trap and misguided effort, wherever it is applied.

In the Second Part, we concentrate mainly on the particularities of various countries. In some places, we have dwelt on a concrete problem in a specific country, for instance salaried women in Mexico, peasant women in Ecuador, the legal status of women in Colombia, or the way the present military regime in Chile has made political use of the traditional image of women. In other cases, we have described the general situation of women, in Puerto Rico, the French Antilles and Uruguay. We have also drawn on the results of an investigation conducted in Matanzas (Cuba) by the Federation of Chilean Women following the elections there, an investigation which highlights the significance of certain traditional conceptions of women and their effect on the participation of women in the country's political life. Other accounts illustrate certain aspects of the Bolivian women's struggle, conditions in a maternity ward in Venezuela, the position of women in El Salvador and the views of a popular leader as to the status of women in Colombia.

We have chosen to produce this book as the work of a

collective primarily because many women have participated directly or indirectly in producing it. Also important was to challenge the misguided sense of power which comes from the very act of writing, and the tendency to take advantage of it in an individualistic way. Not that we believe that individual intellectual work is negative by definition or that it should not receive public recognition. However, in contemporary class society, intellectual activities are inevitably invested with a certain superiority. As a source of privilege, they promote a kind of opportunism which we in no way wish to encourage. We have sought to show that it is quite possible to write as a group and that ideas are no one's private property.

Part One
The Particular Character of Latin American Women's Movements

There are specific characteristics of women's struggles and movements in Latin America which distinguish them from European and North American movements. Women in the so-called 'underdeveloped' countries do have problems similar to those of women in the industrialized countries, in that women in both areas are socially identified as main agents of the reproduction of the dominant ideology as well as of the labour force. However, important differences exist, both in terms of economic development and on the socio-cultural level, which means that the problematic of women is differently structured in each country, embodying characteristics specific to the society in question. In addition to the socio-economic position of women in Latin America, one must also bear in mind the varying degree of influence of indigenous cultures, the extent of women's participation in production and the type of articulation of the different modes of production.

Colonialism and Neo-colonialism

Not only is the Latin American woman oppressed as a woman, she also suffers that loss of identity typical in parts of the world whose main role has been to supply raw materials, first to the colonial metropoles and subsequently to the industrialized countries. In exchange, we receive manufactured goods, films, advertising, fashion magazines and television programmes which introduce different ways of loving and feeling, which deform real needs and replace them with false needs, change values and gradually reinforce existing bonds of economic and cultural dependency, till all our indigenous traditions are suppressed and we are forced to identify with foreign ideological and cultural models. The Spanish culture of the *conquistadores*, marked by seven centuries of Arab-Muslim domination and additionally burdened with Catholicism, introduced sexual stereotypes which capitalism was later to use and develop to its own ends. Women were recognized and valued only as mothers (the Holy Virgin)[1] and lost the high regard and many of the rights they had enjoyed in certain pre-Columbian societies. Labouring under the heritage of Hispanic-Arab and Christian civilization and faced as they are by contemporary underdevelopment and neo-colonialism, Latin American women will have to overcome a great many obstacles before they can liberate themselves.

Machismo

Machismo is often seen as a specifically Spanish and Latin American characteristic. However much it is indeed a basic component of those cultures, it is by no means exclusively Latin. In fact the Spanish word can and has been used to designate a world-wide phenomenon.

Machismo is an expression—sometimes at the level of caricature—of the patriarchal system. It consists in establishing a certain superiority of men over women, by which men feel themselves to be privileged beings, both in society and in the family. This serves to consolidate a certain 'specialization', a division of functions, attitudes, capacities and qualities which are then attributed to one sex or the other. As a counterpart to the *machismo* stereotype of masculinity, the patriarchal system has also developed a stereotype of femininity, the 'female object' or 'female eunuch'.[2] Both implicitly and explicitly, women have been used to the advantage of men.

However, neither men nor women are as individuals consciously aware of the relationship of domination and subordination which has been established between them: on the contrary, they have so internalized and developed it in their attitudes and aspirations that they have come to consider this relationship as a 'natural', 'biological' fact.

Women, defined at every level of society in terms of their reproductive functions, both physical and ideological, have acted as agents in the transmission and diffusion of the patriarchal system's existing stereotypes. Yet the oppression of women is not the result of the 'natural brutishness' of men. To reduce *machismo* to a pure relation between man and woman would be to ignore the fact that cultural stereotypes correspond to a certain economic and social order. The *macho* (male) is himself the victim of a system whose relations of production are constituted by the exploitation of one part of society in order to ensure the domination of a minority and to safeguard that minority's interests.

Because of the historical conditions experienced by our people, weighed down as they are by foreign domination, *machismo* as an ideological expression has acquired certain specific traits in our continent. Like the women, the men of Latin America have been stripped of their identity. As a response to his own alienation, the Latin American male feels himself to be at least the master of 'his' woman, and will often use violence, even physical violence, against her without realizing that by alienating her he increases his own alienation.

Nonetheless, *machismo* is not a local problem; it also affects the industrialized countries, although in more subtle forms which may be more difficult to unmask but which are just as dangerous. In the 'civilized' countries, *machismo* violence is mainly expressed through psychological pressures and the limitations imposed on women at the socio-cultural level.

'Western' values, claiming a universality in whose name colonization can take place, are themselves based on a model of 'male supremacy'. The model relies on an artificial identification of rationality, technique and efficiency with domination itself. In the name of this identification, the 'West' has claimed the right to level and destroy any different form of cultural expression. The resulting history of domination has been a prolongation of the history of man's exploitation of man and of men's domination of women.

The West's cultural values have in practice involved a systematic and complete refusal to recognize women as social, as essential and active participants in the historical process. Male supremacy relies on the fact that historically the activities which were valued by society coincided with the work done by men. For instance, during periods when art, religion or philosophy were given a predominant role in society, they were reserved exclusively for men.

The question here is not that of a particular type of oppressive relationship. It concerns the very bases of oppression, the global and universal fact of domination. Certain tendencies within European and North American feminism continue to define themselves in terms of the structures established by those dominant authorities and structures in which the 'masculine' model is still in force. In other words, this feminism limits women's demand for liberation to a question of personal fulfilment. The struggle thus remains at the level of individual demands, and does not begin to touch upon the social structure from which domination stems. The main problem is allowed to persist; reversing the old values is by no means the same as destroying them. On the contrary, the distorted relations and oppressive violence are simply allowed to continue; the traditional model is reinforced, *hembrismo*[3] replaces *machismo* and genuinely free heterosexuality remains just as inaccessible.

Yet a sense that current heterosexual relations are in general frustrating and synonymous with domination and subordination does not necessarily mean rejecting heterosexuality *per se*. It is after all an essentially human social reality. On the contrary, the first step towards an authentic heterosexuality is the demand for a qualitative transformation of relations between men and women involving a radical change in the male and female attitudes prevalent in the Western culture which has shaped our own countries.

The necessary transformation in relations between men and women should thus not be reduced to an irreconcilable conflict between the sexes. Rather it is a struggle we must wage together if we are to attain a full flowering of our physical, affective, intellectual and creative capacities. In the course of this struggle, women, as the oppressed party, must demand and obtain equitable participation in society. It is women who will play the vanguard role in the transformation of sexual stereotypes and of the patriarchal

9

system within which we all live.

The content of the traditional social relations between men and women can change only within a new system of relations of production. In their turn, these new relations of production will give rise to new social relations and create a space in which a new system of values can develop, values which incorporate elements geared to physical and cultural liberation and opposed to any practice of exploitation, and hence also to the oppression of one sex by the other.

Class Struggle and 'Sisterhood'

The problem of women is so vast and complex that it would be absurd to try to impose directives as to the content and final form of any feminist theory. This theory is still being debated and its development will necessarily require a conscious effort by all women.

The various tendencies which exist in the women's movement have one thing in common—the struggle to liberate women. However, different groups defend opposing theories. We must stop and ask which feminism and what sort of liberation we are talking about, and how we intend to achieve it. These questions can and do already divide the movement into groups which, each in their own way, claim to be working for women's liberation. Those who consider that the main contradiction in society is the specific oppression of women, and therefore base their whole struggle on this contradiction, isolate themselves from any class-based analysis. Although one can talk of a form of oppression common to all women, this oppression does not present itself in the same terms for a bourgeois woman as for a proletarian woman. Any attempt to seek a solution based on idealist principles such as an immutable female solidarity ('sisterhood') according to the postulate 'we are all sisters, all equal', amounts to a utopian denial of the class society in which we find ourselves. The differences between women are in many ways more relevant than the similarities between them.

Solutions based on 'sisterhood' invite us to enter into an imaginary paradise and thus conceal the problem of class struggle and women's role within it. In the final analysis, the essential point is to define the relation between women's struggle for emancipation and the class struggle, or, in more practical terms, the relation between the women's movement and revolutionary political movements.

Defining our Aims

The aims appropriate to a women's struggle in Latin America can only be established in terms of the concrete reality specific to each country. In Latin America generally, the attempt to put forward the goals and practices of women's movements from the industrialized countries can often lead to the formation of a movement from which most of the continent's sub-proletarian, peasant and working-class masses are excluded. Indeed these movements set out neither to defend the interests of the exploited classes nor to fight for a real change in Latin American society. It is thus hardly surprising that neither their demands nor their practices involve the women of the most populous classes.

Some of the demands which are characteristic of the European and North American women's movements cease to have any meaning when they are transposed into a Latin American context.

'Equal Pay for Equal Work'

Let us look at what happens to a demand such as *'equal pay for equal work'* when it is transposed into the Latin American reality. In certain rural areas, especially those with a predominantly indigenous population, there is no salary system like that of a developed capitalist economy. The family functions as a productive unit and receives one overall payment (or part of the crop) in exchange for the work of all its members. The issue of male and female salaries does not arise; we are talking about a pre-capitalist mode of production which is being utilized by the capitalist system.[4] In other cases, women from the underdeveloped countries who are already incorporated into the process of capitalist production are indeed much more exploited than the men, just as they are in the developed world. In Latin

11

America, the most stultifying and boring jobs in manufacturing industry, agriculture, mining and the tertiary sector are usually done by women, and their salaries are lower than the men's. There can be no doubt that the struggle for equal wages is both important and appropriate. The standard of living of many women, some of whom are the main economic providers for their families, could be improved as a result, and this is also a demand appropriate to promoting women's organizations with a view to revolutionary struggle. Obtaining a better salary would definitely constitute progress, although it would not, in itself, amount to a liberation of women. In Latin America today, apart from Cuba, the struggle for equal wages is basically a struggle to be less exploited than at present, to be exploited as much but no more than the men. Since even the men are very highly exploited, higher salaries might make women more equal but would certainly not constitute liberation.

Nursery Schools

The struggle for more nursery schools is meaningless if it is not tied in with an approach to each country's problems in education. Even assuming a certain success, what would happen to the children once they left the nursery, given that even the primary school facilities are so patently inadequate?

Control of Reproduction

In Latin America massive contraception and sterilization programmes are used as a form of imperialist control over the birth rate. Of course, we are not denying the importance of demographic policies worked out according to a country's needs and objectives. The problem arises when one considers a type of control that is imposed from abroad and applied at home by each country's dominant classes under the pretext of the supposed overpopulation of Latin America and the Caribbean. Indeed the *low* population density of Latin American countries has often been presented as one of the obstacles to industrial development.[5] The sterilization programmes are essentially geared towards eliminating or holding back the reproduction of vast sectors of the population (Indians, impoverished peasants, etc.) whose present reproductive rhythm leads to uncontrollable demographic growth. This is why the struggle for the right of all Latin American women to have the children they want is necessary: it involves us in the denunciation of the genocidal policies carried out in many countries under the aegis of the U.S. Government, various multinationals and certain international agencies.[6] Imposed sterility is as much a form of oppression as imposed maternity.

More generally, any struggle aimed at securing free access to the various forms of contraception and greater control over our own bodies must begin by trying to raise the educational level of the population, so that *all* women may decide rationally as to which method of birth control they wish to use.

The legalization of abortion in countries where social security benefits are non-existent or grossly inadequate would only be a measure of liberation for a small minority of women, unless of course it was part of an overall struggle for a better health and sanitation service, available to the population as a whole.

Divorce

The legalization of divorce, or improvements in the relevant laws in countries where it is already legal, is a demand which only affects married women. In many Latin American countries 40 per cent of the population live together unmarried and regard marriage as a luxury reserved for the rich. Because of the irresponsibility inherent in *machismo*, a high percentage of women on low incomes must bring up their children alone, with no legal protection whatsoever.

There are many other examples. Those we have mentioned should be enough to show the serious mistakes which can be made when the goals of the Western women's liberation movement are mechanically transposed from one society to another. We do not wish to deny the contribution European and North American women's movements have made to the Latin American women's struggle, but these contributions must be analysed, subjected to criticism and re-examined in the light of a different economic, political and cultural reality.

In this sense, Latin American women can make an important contribution not just to the movement in the underdeveloped countries, but also to that of the industrialized world, by helping women there to realize the relativity of certain principles which have been considered universal. Latin American women will invent their own forms of struggle, adapted to their own goals.

Perspectives for Struggle

Women's struggle for liberation must be waged on several fronts: in the home, the factory, the countryside and the street. But the priority given to each of these fronts will depend on the concrete circumstances in each country. A genuine women's movement must support and participate in the various efforts made by women to improve their conditions, in the factory, in the trade unions, in the peasant organizations and in every aspect of the social struggle.

Women's solidarity with each of these partial struggles is essential for a movement seeking to liberate women, for it is from such struggles that the women's movement will draw its substance and its *raison d'etre*. In the end, not only will working women be part of the movement, but their tactics and daily practice will provide it with its orientation, and it will then be able to influence the general political process in each country. In this context, it is worth mentioning a few ideas as to how the various sectors of women's activity can be linked together.

In the more industrially developed countries of Latin America, where there are significant numbers of women workers (Argentina, Brazil, Mexico, Puerto Rico),[7] women's organizations within the trade unions will be crucial. Proletarian consciousness grows as workers make demands. During a strike, the supportive intervention of the women's movement could promote a general awareness of the specific oppression of women. Such a struggle might gain a significance extending far beyond that of a simple wage demand.

One thing all our countries have in common is the existence of specific trade union organizations in which, because of the nature of the work, women form the majority—teaching, nursing and the textile industry, for example. Within such organizations, it should be quite possible to engage right now in activities which touch upon the condition of women. There is also a whole range of jobs done mainly by women who are not unionized—servants, seamstresses, pieceworkers and women who prepare foodstuffs at home for sale. Usually they work on their own, which makes unionization more difficult. Bringing these women together would certainly be another appropriate area of action for our feminist movements.

In the countries where agriculture is the main activity, peasant women participate directly in the process of production. This paves the way for large-scale organization amongst these women and for their incorporation as militants in the social struggle. There are many good examples of this already—the land occupations led by women in Bolivia, Peru and Ecuador, and the organizations of peasant women which already exist, in Colombia for instance. A declaration presented to the First Congress of Peasant Women, in Colombia,[8] stressed that the struggle for women's liberation cannot be separated from the struggle to emancipate the exploited classes. 'We do not want to be the slaves of slaves,' they said. The socialist and feminist implications of such a statement highlight the fact that in our continent simultaneous struggles are not only possible but essential. One must also pose the problem of women at home, where women, confined to the family nexus and socially isolated, are generally more difficult to organize.

As a general expression, the term 'housewife' covers a wide range of situations, from the idle bourgeois 'mistress' of a house full of servants to the women who live in shanty towns and who are generally unemployed or part-time workers. The term is most applicable to the 'housewife' who belongs to one of the various strata of the petty bourgeoisie. Her particular conditions usually make her resistant to change and particularly receptive to the values of the dominant ideology. To reach these women, and there are a great many of them, one would have to work out a policy of consciousness-raising based on the environment in which they operate from day to day. Such a policy would have to work on the community level, in terms of housing estates, streets, districts, etc., and through institutions such as the school, parent-teacher associations, adult education institutes, the church, and family planning centres. However all this can only be carried out by women's groups already well implanted in the community, and this itself is by no means usual in Latin America and the Caribbean.

We hold that the liberation of these women can only come about through their direct incorporation into the processes of production, through economic independence and active participation in society. From this point of view, the socialization of domestic tasks will eventually become indispensable and will provide a partial goal around which a great number of women can come together.

Some Conclusions

Most feminist groups in contemporary Latin America and the Caribbean are made up of intellectual women from the petty bourgeoisie or 'middle-class elites' who draw their inspiration from abroad. As a result, they are frequently isolated and often adopt methods and goals of struggle inappropriate to the real needs of most Latin American women. We ourselves, the authors, are not immune from these dangers. Despite our awareness of our own limit-ations, we still believe that a real liberation movement must express the hopes of the majority of women in Latin America. If it is to do so, it must be a popular movement based on a revolutionary praxis.

In each country, the strategy and organization of the women's liberation movement will necessarily depend on the existing socio-economic structure, on the size and influence of the political organizations and, more generally, on the prevailing laws, codes, hygienic and educational conditions affecting the population as a whole and women in particular. The latter aspect is a crucial area of study for any women's organization.

Although we obviously recognize the need to change economic structures if we are to transform the social relations between men and women, we do not think that changing the economic system is in itself sufficient. Ways of thinking change only very slowly so that, in a revolutionary situation, economic change occurs so rapidly that people's frames of reference cannot adjust fast enough. Transformations in the relations of production can and do lead to changes in mental structures, but these changes may take different forms. Old conceptions may be adapted to the new situation, find new forms of expression or even act as a brake on the revolutionary process itself. And this is particularly true of existing attitudes about the relations between men and women, between women and the family, and between women and society as a whole.

The Latin American people's struggle for liberation is both necessary and urgent, but the task of liberating women and transforming the traditional relationship between the sexes must also be undertaken, and right now. Nor can the latter struggle be subordinated to the former, as if they represented successive fronts. Both must be fought simultaneously if an effective victory is to be won.

In fighting for the economic and cultural liberation of their countries, women must also win positions from which they can promote their own liberation. This means fighting for effective participation by women both in the rank and file and in the political leadership of the revolutionary movements. It also means challenging the structures of domination and power relations which tend to persist even within revolutionary struggles.

In this sense, we find indispensable the criticism and self-criticism of certain positions unthinkingly adopted by left-wing (and other) political organizations when dealing with the problems of women. We are referring of course to the conservative and sometimes even reactionary attitude often evident in the day-to-day practice of certain members of revolutionary organizations. Many active militants, who are considered good revolutionaries, continue to impose the old relations of domination and oppression on their women comrades. Indeed, these same individuals frequently denounce the concerns of the women's movement as a diversionary tactic of 'imperialist ideology'.[9] But this reveals a very uncritical stance towards the dominant ideology and traditional values, especially *machismo*. These cannot be seen as part of the national 'folklore' but rather

17

as social practices and values which effectively institution-
alize the specific alienation of women.

Up till now, women have been recognized as wives,
mothers, daughters and even as consumers. What women
today are demanding is to be recognized without qualifying
adjectives. Thus the women's liberation movement, as a
movement specific to women, must be autonomous. The
choice facing these women is not between isolation and
subordination to the political parties. As one liberation
movement amongst many, they must engage in practices of
struggle stemming from a common approach to the overall
aim of liberating our peoples.

Notes

1. In Catholicism, the pure woman is represented by the Virgin
   Mary, the 'immaculate' wife and mother. Virginity as a social
   value divides women into two categories: on the one hand,
   you have 'decent women' who live their sexuality solely as a
   'conjugal duty' and who devote themselves to their home
   and children; on the other, you have the 'street-walking
   prostitutes'.
2. Germaine Greer, *The Female Eunuch*, MacGibbon and Kee:
   London, 1970.
3. *Hembrismo* (domination by women) corresponds to the
   appropriation by women of certain social functions.
4. Indeed, in certain provinces of Northern Argentina, the
   entire family group, irrespective of age or sex, receives an
   overall salary calculated according to the weight in kilos of
   the harvest they present.
5. Comparative (1971–72) figures for population density in
   various other countries (number of inhabitants per square
   kilometre): U.S. 72, France 95, U.K. 228, Germany 239; and
   in Latin America, Bolivia 5, Argentina 8, Colombia 21,
   Mexico 26 (Atlas, 6th edition, Éditions de Poche, Paris,
   1975).
6. One of the conditions frequently set by the World Bank for
   loans to underdeveloped countries is a reduction of the
   birth rate by a given percentage, determined according to

'economic' factors. In his book, *Las Venas Abiertas de America Latina* (Siglo XXXI, Editions S.A., Mexico, 1973), Edward Galeano quotes the following statement by Robert McNamara, President of the World Bank: 'The population explosion is the main obstacle in the path of Latin America's progress. [Therefore] countries which apply birth control programmes will be given priority for World Bank loans.' According to one World Bank document, 'given that a developing country with a *per capita* average income of between U.S. $150 and U.S. $200 a year manages to reduce the population growth rate by 50 per cent over a period of 25 years, its *per capita* income 30 years on will be 40 per cent higher than it would otherwise be, and twice as high after 60 years' (p. 9). '*Per capita* income' is, of course, an abstract category which corresponds to the division of the gross national product by the total number of inhabitants of that country. This theoretical average tells us strictly nothing about the real distribution of income within the population. The case of Mexico is illuminating. In 1969, the poorest 20 per cent of families received only 4 per cent of the country's total income, while the richest 10 per cent of families appropriated 51 per cent. In Brazil, one-third of the national income is concentrated in the hands of 5 per cent of the population, while three-quarters of the people live at subsistence level ('Croissance et contrainte', *Le Monde*, Paris, 23 February 1977). A fall in the rate of population growth may well increase the figure for 'average *per capita* income' but it tells us very little about the real problem. Galeano denounces this policy which 'proposes to sanction a very unequal distribution of income between countries and amongst social classes, and to convince the poor that their poverty is the direct result of all the children who have been born when they could have been avoided' (p. 10).

7. Puerto Rico is in this respect exceptional. For instance, women represent 56 per cent of the work force in manufacturing industry.

8. The first Congress of Peasant Women was held in 1973 in Ovejas in Colombia's Sucre Province.

9. The example of Puerto Rico is worth mentioning. Certain members of left or separatist organizations there have branded feminism as an instrument of imperialist domination. Basing themselves on the idea that feminism diverts people from the struggle for the island's independence, they have put it about that defending *machismo* and the cult of virginity was equivalent to defending the island's culture. While we do not deny that many U.S. feminist movements can be used to divide the people, we utterly reject the idea that the only solution is to defend *machismo* and virginity. The struggle for women's liberation must be linked to the struggle for progress and conducted alongside it.

A Historical Survey

Throughout Latin American history[1] there have been two sorts of women's struggles. On the one hand, there have been women's groups who deliberately ignored the problems of national dependency, who sought to separate women's struggles from class struggles, and who thereby acted as tools of the dominant classes. On the other, there have been women who struggled not only for their own liberation but also for the transformation of the social structures, sometimes with other women and sometimes alongside men.

The first kind of struggle is often focused around the slogan 'we are all sisters'. Indeed for certain European and North American feminist currents this is axiomatic: The postulate of sisterhood was defended at the 1975 World Conference on International Women's Year organized by the U.N. in Mexico.

The idea of sisterhood suggests that proletarian and bourgeois women are closer to each other as women than they are to the men of their own class. Social division is presented primarily and almost exclusively as a division between the sexes. Women supposedly constitute a caste (some have even called it a race) whose main characteristic is their oppression by men, who are therefore the main enemy: if men as a whole hold power, women's struggles must be directed against all of them.

On the other hand, other feminist tendencies start from the fact that we live in a class society. Social classes are not defined in terms of sex, but in terms of the relations between people and the means of production. According to this analysis, the 'female condition' cannot be envisaged homogeneously, as if women in general shared the same situation. The various positions women occupy in the system of production determine, along with other factors, the type of oppression they experience. In fact this oppression is attenuated, accentuated, or in any case expressed differently according to each woman's position in society, in other words according to her social class.

The division of Latin American society into classes is not a new phenomenon. The model imposed by the Spanish colonizers already embodied a division very different from that current in pre-Columbian societies in which both men and women were either exploiters or exploited. Fray Bartolome de Las Casas pointed out long ago that he saw 'one of these ladies whip an Indian girl so hard that the girl died before the lady had a chance to get tired.'[2] Clearly some women exercised power over other women; the control exercised by the colonizers over the colonized was not restricted to men. Nor were these women united simply because they were all women. On the contrary, they were separated by their antagonistic social positions, and those who did hold power used it ferociously.

Confirmation of the existence of class differentiation can be found in the descriptions of women's daily life in Guayaquil (Ecuador) towards the beginning of the 19th Century:

> The wealthier women spent most of their time lying about in hammocks or beds; their only occupation was to give birth to numerous offspring and to supervise the running of the house and the education of the children. They occasionally dispelled the monotony of their lives by chatting with other ladies or with their husbands' guests, by standing at a balcony overlooking an animated street, by going shopping (although never to market), by visiting churches and attending the balls organized from time to time by their marriageable daughters ... For young women of the upper classes, there were only three possible lifestyles: marriage, celibacy or bigotry. They would certainly never demean themselves by working.[3]

By contrast, the less well-off women participated directly in the distribution of goods and services, whether as stallholders, shopkeepers, entertainers, wise women or, inevitably, as prostitutes. Even if they lived alone, their life was an endless round of chores from morning till night. As soon as they started living with a man, with or without the Church's blessing, they had to prepare the meals, do the laundry, clean the floors and bring up the children. The wives of labourers and journeymen helped in the fields, and the wives of artisans toiled in the workshops . . . Working-class women supplemented their husbands' wages. Those who lived alone subsisted as washerwomen, kitchen hands, seamstresses, nannies and servants.[4]

In the 20th Century, the situation is still very much the same. A Venezuelan government measure aimed at fixing a minimum wage for domestic staff encountered stiff opposition, as can be seen from the following magazine article:

'The Servant Problem'

The President really made fools of us when he decreed that *servants* should be paid 15 Bolivars a day on average. Now the *servants* no longer wish to work in a home. As soon as they can *speak*, they try to get a job in an office. If this goes on, the servants will be *living better* than their mistresses. Already they earn far more than they're worth. They get a *house, food,* a *telly* and a *radio*, the best *food* in the house, *clean linen* and other specialities. But the moment it comes to working, it becomes apparent that *these servants* have not the faintest idea about what needs to be done. They go off on a Saturday morning and come back only on Sunday evening, or even sometimes on Monday. From now on the Government will be giving them a *special identity card* to show when they apply for a job. This will make them even more *bigheaded*. Perhaps this is yet another instance of *world inflation*. In short, any family which cannot pay a *good salary* will *really be stuck*. On top of it all, these so-called servants *pinch* anything they can lay their hands on, and when one realizes a few months later what has happened, there is nobody to turn to. Please Mr. President . . . be fair to the housewife who has to cope with these 'untouchables'.[5]

The point is not to deny men's domination over women but to characterize it and situate it within the overall social context as a factor which guarantees the continued existence of the capitalist system of exploitation.

Early Women's Struggles

Just as the division of society into classes can be concealed behind appeals to 'sisterhood', so can the fact of women's active participation in various struggles, even before the Conquest and certainly before feminist ideas appeared in Latin America:

> There is a parallel between the way bourgeois history has tried to hide the predominant role played by class conflict in the evolution of society and the way women's struggles have been interpreted as isolated events divorced from contemporaneous social struggles.[6]

This is because:

> The bureaucrats who write up the history of women's participation in social movements use texts, memoirs and other documents to present a static picture full of heroines and famous women, a picture which stresses their subordinate condition, their sacrifices, their self-denial and the support they provided for their husbands' struggles. The real meaning and context of these women's actions is thus totally obscured.[7]

But some facts cannot be completely swept under the carpet. In 1778 Baltazara Chuiza led the Guano (Ecuador) rebellion against the Spanish; when they captured her, she was drawn and quartered. In 1781, Bartolina Siza, the wife of Tupac Kapari and one of the first women to fight for independence in Upper Peru (modern Bolivia), organized the siege of La Paz. In 1780, along with her husband, Tupac Amaru, Micaela Bastidas led the most widespread and important revolt against the Spanish Empire and the Viceroy of Peru. Micaela participated actively in the organization and leadership of this struggle. In a letter to her husband dated 6 December 1780, she speaks of her problems and anxieties on the battlefront:

> I have already asked you not to tarry in villages where there
> is nothing to be done; but you carry on with your travels
> without realizing that our soldiers are short of supplies . . .
> and that all the people I have called upon for the descent on
> Cuzco may abandon us . . . . I am not afraid of dying, but I
> tremble for the fate of this poor family so desperately in
> need of help . . . I am ready to march with our people.[8]

In 1780, in what is now Colombia, Manuela Beltran rose
up against the Spanish and led the popular struggle of the
communeros who had revolted against excessively high taxes.
Soon afterwards, in 1803 Lorenza Avemanay, an Indian
from Chimborazo Province in what is today Ecuador, led
another major revolt against the Spanish *conquistadores* in
Guamote.

Although few women participated *directly* in the 19th
Century wars of independence, many contributed actively
to the resistance networks. In Bolivia, Juana Azurduy was
one of the first to sound the call to arms for independence
in Latin America. She participated in the guerrilla wars
against the Spanish in the Chucusaca area from 1809 to
1825. In 1817, Policarpa Salavarrieta was shot in Bogota
(Colombia) for having been a 'liaison agent' in the
liberation struggle. In 1819, Antonia Santos was shot in
Socorro (Santander), Colombia, for the same reason. In
Ecuador, women helped the rebel army considerably, not
only carrying out all the traditional women's work
(cooking, washing, care of the wounded, etc.) but hiding
weapons, running intelligence networks and even engaging
in physical combat in certain battles. The most famous of
these women were Manuela Saenz and Rosa Campusano, to
whom San Martin gave the Order of the Sun at Lima, along
with Manuela Canizares, Rosa Montufar, and others.

But 'independence' from Spain did not alter the
precarious living conditions of the majority of the
population, especially not that of the women. The colonial
economic structure remained almost intact in Ecuador as
well as in Colombia, Peru and Bolivia, etc.

At the end of the 19th Century, during the great miners'
strikes in Chile, the women organized themselves into
women's committees to promote the 'unlit ovens' (*cocinas
apagadas*) strike: when the strikers came home to eat, they

were thus pressured into going back to the mine to
continue the strike. The women thereby prevented the
miners from giving in and actively stimulated the struggle.

The Absence of a Suffragette Movement

During the 19th Century in Latin America, there was no
equivalent of the European and North American suffragette
movements. We need to know why. There are of course
many reasons, which cannot all be dealt with here, but we
can at least put forward certain working hypotheses.
Further work on the subject is needed.

The Political Reasons

At this time many Latin American countries had only just
obtained their independence and were devoting their
efforts to building up national societies with their own
identities. Furthermore, in many of them, complex internal
power struggles were being waged. There were also
frequent external wars, for instance between Brazil and the
La Plata provinces (1825–28), between Chile and Argentina
on one side and Bolivia and Peru on the other (1836–48),
between Paraguay and the triple alliance of Brazil,
Argentina and Uruguay (1865–70)[9] and between Peru, Chile
and Bolivia (1879–83).

The Economic Reasons

The new Latin American countries retained their traditional
economies: until independence, they provided Spain and
Portugal with raw materials; later they supplied Europe,
(especially Britain and France), and the U.S.

The Social Reasons

To begin with, slavery persisted as a practice in many
countries during the 19th Century. In Brazil, it was not
formally abolished until 1888.[10] Furthermore, although
there were many slave revolts, there were no abolitionist
movements comparable to those in the U.S.
  In the industrialized countries, in contrast, there were
many factors influencing the growth of a women's suffrage
movement, notably the incorporation of women into

productive labour, the development of female education, increasing urbanization and the spread of birth control. In Latin America, things were very different. Women only entered productive manufacturing industry at the end of the 19th Century, for instance. Even the women of the dominant classes were still relatively uneducated, bound by religion and centred on the home (the only vocation allowed to women by the Hispanic culture of their countries).

It is thus hardly surprising that the great battles for women's suffrage, so characteristic of 19th Century Europe and the U.S., only emerged in Latin America during the first decades of the 20th Century.

Mrs. Chapman Catt, the American President of the International Alliance for Women's Suffrage, once declared that, apart from the Spanish American republics, there were only seven independent states in the whole world which did not have an organized movement campaigning for women's right to vote.[11] This is surely an index of the level of resistance to a movement which, for the reasons outlined above, could not develop internally and thus could only come from outside, at a time when any ideas which looked like foreign imports were being actively rejected.

Women's Movements Established

Mexico (1)

In Mexico, women became part of the productive industrial labour force during the second half of the 19th Century, in towns such as Pueblo, Veracruz, Mexico City, etc. Their salaries were lower than men's and employers preferred to hire married women with children because they could be forced to accept fourteen- and eighteen-hour days and negligible salaries paid in kind.[12]

In Mexico, women's struggles apparently focused at this stage mainly on the right to work. Most of these struggles took place towards the end of the 19th Century, but there were a few battles in the late 18th Century. For instance, Adelina Zendejas tells us that 'the tobacco workers called many strikes in Mexico and Veracruz, the main tobacco centres. These women revolted first against the Viceroy, then during the Republic.'[13]

Industrialization of the country as a whole really began in the 1870s but already in 1857 the first major textile strike had paralyzed the industry in Guadalajara. Eighty per cent of the *saraperos* (weavers) were women, and many of them participated in the demand for wage increases and a shorter working day. In 1862 a textile workers' manifesto reiterated these demands and also called for protection for child labourers. Women were already members of the mutual aid groups which later became part of the *Circulos Obreros*.[14]

Women in Mexico clearly played an active part in working-class organizations, and did so as workers themselves, rather than as the wives of workers as in Chile. It was a woman, Carmen Huerta, who in 1880 presided over the Second Workers' Congress. The level of exploitation and the conditions at work were bad enough to provoke major strikes as early as 1881. On the whole the strikes were lost, but they did allow for a radicalization, a raised level of consciousness and, eventually, a higher level of organization, as in the *Hijas de Anahuac* movement which brought together women from the textile and spinning industries of Magdalena, Santa Teresa and Tizapan.[15] From the end of the 19th Century, we find women writing for the Mexican revolutionary papers. For instance in San Luis Potosi, Dolores Jimenez y Muro wrote in *El Libertario* and *Tierra y Justicia* under the pseudonym Espartaco, and, in Parral, Juana Gutierrez de Mendoza edited *La Voz de Ocampo*. Many of these women went to prison during the dictatorship of Porfirio Diaz (1876–1906) and there, too, they organized, taking the name *Hijas de Cuauhtemoc*, and linking up the revolutionary class struggle with women's struggles for civil and political rights. This group later became *Regeneracion et Concordia*, and adopted a programme calling for improvements in the living conditions of the Indians, promotion of the economic, moral and intellectual development of women, equal rights and the alliance of all Mexican revolutionaries.[16]

During the same period, in 1870, the *Siempre-Viva* feminist society appeared and set out to educate women. From 1875 onwards, shortly after women gained access to the teaching profession, small groups of educated women, mainly teachers, began to organize themselves and publish popular pamphlets about women's problems. As early as 1833, groups of women had demanded education for women. The liberal constitution of 1857 incorporated a response to this demand as well as a law on civil divorce. In Puerto Rico, even in the 19th Century, a group of women from the land-owning classes had emerged to press women's right to education. Notable amongst them were Alejandrina Benitez de Gautier, Lola Rodriguez de Tio, Maria Bibiana Benitez, Ana Otelo Fidela Matheu, Francisca Vilella and Belen Zequeira. An Association for the Education of Women was formed to pay for the schooling of poorer girls.[17] The struggle for equal opportunity in education began in 1856, when journals and publications such as *La Guirnalda Puertorriquena* (1856–57) and *La Azucena* (1870) were written exclusively for women, albeit by two men, Ignacio Guasp and Alejandro Tapia y Rivera.

Argentina

In Argentina, one can trace the beginnings of the women's movement back to 1823, when a benevolent society of well-to-do women was started. The Minister who delivered the inaugural address declared that:

> The social existence of women is too vague and uncertain, everything concerning women is still arbitrary. It is essential to improve women's education and to find ways of satisfying their needs, through laws which will lay down their rights and duties. This imperfection in the civil code has been as much of an obstacle to progress as war and fanaticism.[18]

In 1830, *La Argentina*, the 'first women's paper published in La Plata',[19] appeared, followed in 1852 by *La Camelia*, subtitled 'Equality between the Sexes'. Towards the end of the 19th Century, there also emerged groups of socialist women, who organized working women's struggles, especially in the textile and tobacco industries during the first years of the 20th Century. It was also in Argentina that the first organized Latin American women's movements appeared, early in the 1900s.

Why in Argentina? Between 1895 and 1914 it was the country which received the largest wave of immigration,

mainly Italians, Germans and Spaniards. Thus in the big
Argentinian towns with over 100,000 inhabitants, more
than a third of the population was foreign.[20] Also, one
should remember that British influence, predominant
throughout Latin America, was particularly strong in
Argentina, a British financial colony. Britain built the
railroads, ports and light industry and set up refrigeration
units in what was already a major meat-producing country.

One of the first consequences was the opening up of the
liberal professions to bourgeois women. Cecilla Grierson,
the first woman doctor in Argentina, attended the
International Women's Congress in 1899 and delivered the
following message:

> Women's work will be strengthened by the energetic efforts
> of the women involved in this International Congress. When
> we have a National Women's Council in our own country, it
> will be clear for all to see that, in Argentina, women are the
> main pillars of our religion, the vanguard of social purity,
> refined manners, elegance and domestic happiness, and that
> they can, at the same time, carry out many good works.[21]

And it was indeed these educated well-to-do women who,
in 1900, set up the National Council of Argentinian
Women, which affiliated in 1901 to the International
Council of Women, a body established in 1888 by the
North American women's suffrage movements in order to
bring together 'women of all nations . . . to ensure the
prosperity of the family and the state'.[22] The National
Council of Argentinian Women was fundamentally nothing
more than the continuation of that first 'Benevolent
Society' founded in 1823; it was certainly never a militant
pressure group. These women's organizations consisted of
elites whose main interests were European literature and
charity work and who were no more concerned with
political rights in Argentina than were their equivalents
anywhere else in Latin America.

In 1910, the National Council of Women organized the
first Latin American Women's Congress in Buenos Aires.
For the first time, representatives from all the Latin
American countries gathered together and met representatives of feminist movements from Italy, Austria, Germany,

Spain, Switzerland and the U.S. The first concrete link between Latin American women and the women's suffrage movement had been forged.

The Argentinian women's movement began as an organization of bourgeois women involved in charity work and cultural activities.[23] Then in 1918, Julieta Lanteri founded the National Feminist Party, of which she became president. When she tried to stand for election as a Deputy, however, she was not allowed to do so on the grounds that she was not registered in her constituency. Argentinian women had to wait till 1951 before they obtained universal suffrage.

Mexico (2)

In Mexico, the women's movement really took off from 1906 onwards, on the basis of demands for civil and voting rights. Women of every social class had participated in the struggles of the Mexican Revolution. Peasant women accompanied their men, not only in order to carry out 'feminine' tasks such as 'fetching and pounding the maize, making the *tortillas*', 'carrying the ammunition and all the other instruments necessary to the mobilization', but also to participate in combat.[24] Teachers, students and women of every profession worked in the hospitals, organized revolutionary propaganda and fought on the battlefields. Some of them even became officers and commanded combat troops.

Despite their contribution, the 1917 Constitution did not give women the vote, on the pretext that theirs had not been a collective movement with this aim in mind:

> Mexican women have traditionally concentrated their activities on the home and the family. Women have no political consciousness and do not feel the need to participate in public life, as is shown by the absence of any collective movement to attain this end.[25]

In 1915, a Mexican women's congress was held in Yucatan, the same area in which the *Ligas de Orientacion Femenina* were to emerge to call for land law reform, insisting that stakes in land be allocated irrespective of sex. They also demanded equal salaries, trade union rights, birth control, protection of maternity rights and the abolition of the term 'love child'. The demand for birth control was something very new at the time. Even the most radical women's movements in Europe and the U.S. had not gone that far. These Mexican women's organizations established themselves locally, and in certain states (Yucatan, Chiapas, Tabasco) they won equality before the law, the right to vote and the right to be elected.[26]

In 1931, a Congress Against Prostitution was held, with the aim of abolishing the law which made prostitution a profession. In 1935, the *Frente Unico Proderechos de la Mujer* launched its programme of demands, which included the right to vote and be elected to the National Assembly, equality before the law, and reforms in the Agrarian Law. In fact the Congress took up the demands of the *Ligas de Orientacion Femenina* and, apparently for the first time, called for the integration of Indian women into the social and political movement. The *Frente* also brought together women of every social class—peasants, employees, teachers, intellectuals and professionals.

A few years later, in 1933, the Workers' and Peasants' Congress established a programme for feminist struggle in Mexico and a campaign for the right to vote, for the extension of the *Ley Federal de Trabajo* (federal labour law), for social security benefits, for creches and for the protection of maternity rights. According to some authors, this was the first really feminist programme in Mexico.[27]

Under the Cardenas Presidency (1934–40), women's movements were encouraged by the government which also took measures in their favour such as facilitating access to public office and granting the vote to women militants in the National Revolutionary Party. In 1937 women voted in the election of the Party's candidate for the Chamber of Deputies. The candidate was a woman editor, the widowed mother of six children. The *Frente* put forward its own candidate, its General Secretary. Both women were elected, but since the Constitution included no provision for women's entry into the Chamber, they were not able to exercise their mandate as Deputies. The following year a reform of the Constitution, endorsed by most of the states of Mexico, made it possible for women to serve as Deputies. Between 1936 and 1938, women employed by the state began to organize; they won maternity rights and the first two creches were established.[28]

With the departure of Cardenas, a whole era in Mexican life came to a close. The *Frente* lost its *raison d'etre* and dissolved itself. Its General Secretary died of starvation a few years later, completely forgotten, as were all the other militant women in the *Frente*. The movement, which had played a very major role throughout the 1930s, was completely annihilated.[29] History repeated itself once again: the women who had participated so actively in the profound social and political upheavals which had shaken Mexico and who had expressed their demands so vehemently were forced back into the home.

Uruguay

In Uruguay, a National Council of Uruguayan Women was founded in Montevideo in 1916. Its two main objectives were votes for women and the abolition of the white slave trade; at the time, Montevideo was the main point of entry for women abducted in Europe, who were then sent all over Latin America as white slaves.

The National Council published a journal called *Accion Femenina*, to promote the cause of women's suffrage. As early as 1917, the Uruguayan National Assembly had set up a commission enquiring into the possibilities of a bill to enfranchise women. But the law was not passed until 1932 and was put into operation for the first time during the 1938 elections. In 1919 a purely suffragette association emerged, the Uruguayan Alliance for Women's Suffrage. The Suffrage Commission of the National Women's Council participated in the Alliance, and the Council provided financial assistance, but it remained a totally independent body.

The National Council seems to have functioned as a co-ordinating centre for all the women's organizations; for instance it included delegates from the telephonists, the nurses, the blind and the students. The Council also maintained links with other women's movements in Latin America. Dr. Paulina Luisi, President of the National Council, was invited to Argentina by the *Union Feminista Nacional* in Buenos Aires.[30] While she was there, she met the President of the International Alliance for Women's

Suffrage who, between December 1922 and January 1923, visited Brazil, Chile, Peru, Uruguay, Paraguay and Panama in order to set up a Pan-American Women's Organization.

Ecuador

In Ecuador, the liberal Constitution of 1896–97 declared that, to be allowed to vote, a person must be 'over 21 and able to read and write', and thereby opened the gates of citizenship to women. Article 13 of the 1928–29 Constitution specifically recognized the civil rights of women. Ecuador was thus the second American country, after the U.S., to recognize women's right to vote.

Colombia

Colombia, unlike many other Latin American countries such as Mexico, Uruguay, Brazil, Cuba or Puerto Rico, had no major tradition of organized women's struggles. Nonetheless women were constant participants in the struggles which have marked the history of Colombia, both in the towns and countryside. It is worth noting the isolated but remarkable example of Maria Cano whose actions as a committed militant in the popular struggles of 1925–30 had deep national repercussions. This Colombian journalist and agitator travelled the length and breadth of the country several times over, mobilizing crowds to demonstrate against the crushing hold of the U.S. companies, the anti-democratic laws promulgated by the authorities, the systematic repression of women workers and peasants, and the repeated massacres of strikers.[31]

But despite the active role played by women, especially proletarian women, the question of their participation in social and political struggle was never posed with an explicit consciousness of their condition as women and of the economic, social and cultural conditions which had been imposed upon them. Hence the possibility of organizing a feminist movement never emerged.

Generally speaking, the dominant classes in Colombia considered women as 'instruments' of the existing political authorities. The right to vote, for instance, was not won through a struggle but granted, very late (1957), by the bourgeoisie precisely when it was felt that such a measure would secure the interests of the dominant classes.

The first attempts at a law on women's suffrage were presented and rejected several times, first in 1944 (Albert Lleras), then in 1946 (Augusto Ramirez Moreno, German Zea Hernandez, Gilberto Viera), and again in 1947 (Roberto Urdaneta Arbelaez). It was not until 1954, during the dictatorship of General Gustavo Rojas Pinilla, that a bill on women's suffrage was finally passed. It was applied for the first time in 1957 (Article 1 of the Plebiscite Reform)[32] following the overthrow of Rojas Pinilla. Ironically, this electoral legislation established by the military regime was used against it to consolidate the power of the new rulers. Women were finally able to use their right to vote when the two traditional parties seized power after Rojas' fall and called on the female voters to legitimize the new regime in the ensuing plebiscite.

Brazil

In Brazil, a Brazilian Federation for the Advancement of Women was founded in 1922 by Dr. Berta Luz, with Mrs. Chapman Catt as its official patron. A league for the intellectual emancipation of women had already been set up in 1919. By contrast, the Federation's statutes laid down its aims as follows: to promote women and improve the labour laws affecting them, to obtain political rights for them and to prepare them to exercise those rights, to establish the closest possible friendly links with women's organizations in other countries and *to develop social ties and co-operation amongst women*.

The Federation's most intense agitation focused on women's right to vote. They won a partial victory in 1927, when the State of Northern Rio Grande passed an electoral law entitling all citizens who met the legal requirements to vote and be elected irrespective of sex. But women's right to vote was not actually made part of the Constitution until 1934. However, by 1933, a woman had already been elected to the National Assembly for the first time in Latin America. The new Deputy was Dr. Carlota Pereira y Queiroz.

Also in 1934, under the Vargas Presidency, there emerged a more politically committed organization, the Women's Union, which could count amongst its members as many intellectuals as workers. When Vargas launched the dictatorial phase of his administration many Union members were arrested for opposing the regime.

The Federation of Brazilian Women organized several big congresses attended by delegates from nearly all the Latin American countries. The Federation established branches in every state in Brazil and maintained close links with women's movements abroad.[33]

Cuba

In Cuba, the National Feminist Party founded by Amelia Mallen, who was later to edit the Havana journal *Luz*,[34] already had about 10,000 members by 1914. Their programme included the following:[35] a reform of municipal legislation; a special quota of state jobs reserved for women and open access to all posts in primary education; access to all commercial and industrial jobs and equal wages for women; access to every type of education; economic emancipation through legal reform; absolute equality of civil rights; political equality.

In 1921, eleven organizations, representing some 9,000 women in all, regrouped themselves in a National Federation of Women's Associations and launched a major press and cinema campaign to obtain voting rights for women. Successive Presidents of the Chamber were bombarded with delegations demanding agricultural colleges for women, education for women convicts and greater teaching opportunities in general.

The Federation organized its first national congress in Havana in 1923, with representatives from every women's organization in the country and from many foreign women's movements as well. Resolutions passed called for the intensification of the struggle for women's suffrage and equal civil rights, for 'popular education in civics, so as to consolidate our nationalism,' and an end to prostitution and the white slave trade. Yet despite the struggles of these women, much of their programme remained moribund for several decades. During the Machado dictatorship, the women's movement split into two tendencies sometime between 1925 and 1928. The original reformist current now faced another defined in terms of the political perspectives developed by the revolutionary workers' and students' movements of that time.

Puerto Rico

In Puerto Rico, in 1917, Ana Roque de Duprey founded the Puerto Rican Women's League, the country's first feminist organization, which established branches in San Juan, Ponce and Arecibo.[36] The League called on the Assembly to grant the right to vote to 'women who know how to read and write'. Later, in 1921, the League changed its name to the Social Suffrage League and managed to get new women's suffrage projects presented before the Legislative Assembly (the first bill on the subject had been put forward in 1921) although none were passed. The women of the League then went to Washington and asked the North American authorities to take an interest in women's suffrage. In 1929, literate Puerto Rican women over twenty-one were given the right to vote, a right which remained unexercised until 1932. The educational requirements were finally lifted in 1936.

Parallel to this bourgeois women's struggle for voting rights, a working women's struggle was steadily developing as more and more women entered manufacturing industry. From 1904 onwards, women workers began to participate in the workers' movement. Women's groups such as the Puerta de Tierra Ladies Union, the Lady Workers of Guayama, the Arecibo Sorters and the Ponce Domestic Staff Union were set up within the early trade unions. Later 'women workers played an active role in the Federation of Free Labour and in the creation of the Socialist Party in 1916'.[37] The Party demanded the right to vote for both men and women. Its rules stipulated that at least one-third of the members of any local branch had to be women.

Women played a very important role in the Puerto Rican workers' movement. The bitterest struggles against North American military power and other capitalist interests were in fact waged by women, in the clothing and tobacco industries. Throughout the 1930s women took to the streets to organize strikes, trade unions and political campaigns, both in the towns and in the countryside. These Puerto Rican women workers completely rejected the image of the fragile, weak, pure and passive 'ideal woman'. Many of them distinguished themselves in the workers' struggle, notably Concha Torres, Paca Escabi de Pena, Francisca Andujar, Juana Colon, Luisa Capetillo and

Tomasa Yupart, amongst others.

The Movements Today

In this section, we refer to only some of the countries of Latin America. This should not be taken to mean that women's organizations do not exist in the countries we do not mention but only that we have not been able to gather sufficient information on them. Most of the work in this field is still to be done, first and foremost by gathering some systematic data. All we can do at present is to provide a brief summary of the development of some movements in certain countries.

Bolivia

In Bolivia, the Union of Bolivian Women (U.M.B.O.) was founded on 20 March 1963 to act as an independent body bringing together women from various social strata (housewives, workers, teachers, students, etc.). In May 1966, U.M.B.O. organized its first conference in La Paz. The delegates included many mineworkers' wives from Catavi, Huanuni and Siglo XX as well as women trade union leaders. Article IV of the Congress's Declaration of Intent states that:

> As part of the complex process by which peoples win their freedom, women must ally themselves with or become militants within the political parties which support the struggle to liberate classes and social groups oppressed by capitalism, throughout the world.

Article V recognizes the need for women to organize a movement of their own 'without abandoning their role as militants within their chosen parties. Women must use women's organizations as a very important auxiliary means to study the problems which are *inherent in their own natures*.' But this is an unsatisfactory way of defining the question of women's participation in society. As far as we are concerned, this aspect of the struggle cannot be treated as a mere 'auxiliary'. Nor should the specific problems women face be seen as 'inherent to their natures'; on the contrary, these problems should be treated as an expression of the conditions to which women are socially subjected.

U.M.B.O. fights for the political and civil rights of the entire population, while maintaining links with international women's movements. Forced to remain underground, however, it cannot send delegates to the various congresses and meetings as representatives of the majority of women.

Other Bolivian women are organized in the very different Central Co-ordination Committee for Women's Voluntary Patriotic Action. Their demands include compulsory military service for women and the establishment of a bureau of women's affairs to co-ordinate and plan a methodical and objective programme of voluntary work which would 'integrate all Bolivian women'. For decades women in Bolivia have been organized mainly in trade unions, despite the repression exercised by successive governments. Nonetheless, official groups like this Committee can sometimes put forward some of the goals of the women's movement. For instance, they also call for creches, canteens and communal laundries, and they fight against the use of women as sex objects. To take another example, during International Women's Year, the established authorities set up a range of government bodies. A presidential decree set up a Women's Bureau charged with the official celebration of Bolivian Women's Year. The Bureau, which was part of the Ministry of Social Security and Public Health, was to handle all activities connected with the celebrations, and it was even announced that 'any disobedience or avoidance of the Decree's stipulations would be severely punished'. This amounted to entrusting the International Women's Year activities to 'society ladies' who would not be likely to pose anything like feminist demands and who would certainly not include the exemplary struggles of Bolivian women workers and peasants in their programme.

Venezuela

In Venezuela there are various official women's groups such as the advisory Women's Commission, which is attached to the President's office, the Association of Venezuelan Women and a few other groups attached to political parties such as Women's Movement of the M.A.S.

(Movement towards Socialism) which was, in 1973, one of the first parties to take an interest in women's issues and which organized a Women's Congress in Caracas.

Under the auspices of International Women's Year, a Venezuelan Committee emerged and, in association with the Women's Commission, organized the official First Venezuelan Women's Congress in 1975, which was held in the Caracas Hilton. The goals set out for the event included 'analysis of the situation faced by Venezuelan women and investigation into the worries, aspirations and needs of women from every part of the country, as specified in the prepared topics'.[38] Amongst the topics considered were the legal status of Venezuelan women, their social condition and development, as well as the position of women worldwide.

Autonomous movements have also emerged, for instance the Movement for a New Woman, a study group which publishes a journal containing analyses of the problems of Venezuelan women, particularly working women. It is worth noting that, during International Women's Year, the Movement for a New Woman issued an article denouncing the reformist character of the Women's Commission attached to the President's office. The Movement explained that the Commission and other similar government bodies were merely 'a way of holding back the growing impetus of the women's liberation movement, in that the radical content of women's liberation is reduced to the level of a reformist problematic'.[39]

Colombia

In Colombia there is an official body known as the Union of Colombian Women Citizens. This voluntary body defines itself as 'a non-party, civic and political women's organization which supports democracy and the participation of all Colombians in the government of the country'.[40] Another group, the Organization of Peasant Women, has set itself the goal of winning for women a measure of real democratic participation in production and social and cultural affairs. The Organization's first Congress was held in 1973 and has established links with women in other sectors, focusing mainly on agrarian issues, educational and health needs, the concrete problems of women, and the role they should play in the development of the struggle for social change generally. Further study groups are beginning to spring up as well.

Ecuador

In Ecuador several women's organizations have been active since 1963, but most of them have set out to organize middle-class and petty-bourgeois women around a few 'women's' demands appropriate to their class interests. There was no exclusively women-only structure in which working-class women could organize relatively autonomously until 1975 when the *Comite Femenino de Solidaridad con las Conflictas Laborales* was formed. This Committee, which was made up mainly of women workers and students from working-class areas, emerged at a time when class struggle was intensifying in Ecuador. It aimed principally to provide support for the strike movement and to reinforce working-class unity.

In June 1976, the Women's University Brigades were formed. Responding to the idea that 'the University must serve the people', they tried to establish much closer ties between the University and the working-class sectors. As opposed to bureaucratic or bourgeois organizations and in contrast to the various government bodies attempting to organize working-class 'mothers' in Women's Circles, the Brigades set out to link women's problems and popular struggles.

Brazil

In Brazil, during International Women's Year, a seminar on 'the role and behaviour of Brazilian women' was organized by the United Nations Information Centre in Brazil and by the Brazilian Press Association. The most fruitful result was the setting up of a Brazilian Women's Centre in Rio. Given the political situation in present-day Brazil, the Centre had to provide itself with very precise statutes: it is illegal for more than ten people to get together unless it is within some legally sanctioned framework. Under the umbrella of the Centre, a very diverse set of workshops and study groups was formed.

Despite the difficulties of reaching the vast, exploited and politically marginalized female population of the country, the proliferating women's groups are beginning to have an impact on Brazilian life. They have successfully denounced the discriminatory practices of many large firms, such as PETROBAS, the state oil company which refused to employ women engineers. They have proposed reforms in the laws affecting women, which are currently being studied (1977). Every aspect of the labour laws has been carefully examined, and certain restrictions, supposedly designed to protect women, have been exposed as means of hiding real problems in the labour market. For instance, women were not allowed to work in civil engineering until the shortage of 'manpower' provoked by low wages resulted in women being hired to fill the most unskilled jobs.

Mexico

In Mexico, women have continued to play a major role in the people's struggle despite the setbacks of the 1940s and after. To take only a couple of recent examples, one could look at the strike for better working conditions organized by ticket collectors on the Underground in Mexico City or the telephonists' strike in 1976. Also, between 1968 and 1971 women took an active role in the student movement; many of them were leaders and subsequently arrested.[41] In general, the political climate from the early 1970s onwards encouraged the re-emergence of women's groups. In 1972 there were already several consciousness-raising and study groups meeting regularly in various districts of Mexico City. Towards the end of the year, the results of these investigations began to reach a wider public through articles in the local press, pamphlets and leaflets. Many meetings were organized and the *Mujeres en Accion Solidaria* group was especially active during this period.

But differences in the conception of women's problems very quickly led to splits and the emergence of new groups, especially from 1974 onwards. Some of these were co-opted and incorporated by the so-called 'official' organizations,[42] for instance women in the liberal professions who remained affiliated to their respective associations while waiting for an opportune moment to secure some form of public office.

International Women's Year had a lasting and positive

impact. The publicity surrounding the event sensitized many women to the issues involved; books and articles were published on the subject and the convictions of many revolutionary women were in fact strengthened. *FEM* and *La Revuelta*, two journals published by women, came out in late 1976.

There were many groups who argued that the oppression and exploitation of women were inseparable from the economic system and the specific historical conditions of the country: notably the *Grupo Femenil Popular*; the *Grupo de la Coordinacion de Organizaciones e Instituciones Progresistas*, which organized a women's section in the *Partido Popular Socialista* (P.P.S.); a women's section in the railwayworkers trade union; the *Union Nacional de Mujeres Mexicanas*; the women involved in the *Universidad Obrera,* and those in the *Associacion de Egresados de Escuelas para Hijas de Trabajadores.*[43] Peasant women as well organized themselves around local problems and projects for co-operative work.

Now that the problem of abortion has become a national issue, and despite very divergent opinions on the subject, a majority of women's groups have managed to unite on this issue in order to press their demands. The campaign for legalized abortion has mobilized women of many different tendencies, including the *Movimento de Liberacion de la Mujer*, the *Movimento Nacional de Mujeres A.C.,* the *Jovenes Revolucionarias*, the *Programa Mexico-Ano Internacional de la Mujer*, the *Tribuna y Accion de la Mujer*, the *Consejo de Mujeres de Mexico*, the *Grupo de Doctoras del Hospital de la Mujer*, etc.

Puerto Rico

In 1952, Puerto Rico became one of the first countries in the world to include in its Constitution an Article specifically outlawing discrimination on grounds of sex. Nonetheless, discrimination persisted. In 1973 a government commission was set up to improve women's rights at work and elsewhere. One of its aims was to encourage all activities which would help Puerto Rican women secure equal opportunities in education and enable them to occupy even the most senior posts in the running of the country's affairs, be it in the state sector or in private business.

The Federation of Puerto Rican Women is one

organization which defines itself explicitly in terms of working-class women's interests. In many respects, its position is close to that of the Puerto Rican Socialist Party. The Federation publishes a feminist journal entitled *Women's Words*. Very different is the *Mujer Integrate Ahora* group (M.I.A., 'Women Unite Today') which rejects any party political influence. The group's journal is significantly called *El Talon de la Chancleta* ('The Heel of the Slipper').[44] Working-class combativity and organization are in general on the increase in Puerto Rico and women have joined in the upsurge, organizing themselves into a Confederation of Working Women's Representatives.

Cuba

In Cuba, shortly after the 1959 Revolution, the new government set about improving the living conditions of women; indeed the emancipation of women was a government priority. Only a month after the Revolution, Fidel Castro was heard to say, 'Yes, racial discrimination is a subject which must be discussed, but so is discrimination against women.'[45] On 23 April 1960 the Federation of Cuban Women was set up. Its task was not only to organize women and promote their entry into production but also to encourage their ideological, political and cultural education so as to accelerate Cuban women's incorporation into the social life of the country, thereby stimulating the revolutionary process. The Federation soon became a mass organization with 2,051,906 members in its 46,425 branches, representing some 77 per cent of the country's female population over the age of fourteen.[46] It is a member of the International Democratic Federation of Women and already represented in the United Nations Commission on the Legal and Social Status of Women.

Finally, throughout Latin America, there are women's groups strongly influenced by the big feminist movements from abroad (notably the North American N.O.W.). Their activities in canvassing for broad support on the basis of general demands fail, as we have already mentioned, in that they do not take into account the specificity of the women's struggle in each country.

The Mexico Conference

This chapter would not be complete without some reference to a recent event which has been claimed as marking a turning point in the history of women throughout the world and in Latin America in particular. The event in question is the World Conference on International Women's Year held in Mexico from 19 June to 2 July 1975 under the auspices of the U.N.

Without going into the history, political content or eventual effectiveness of the proposals presented by the various delegations to the Conference, we would like to focus briefly on the apparently contingent fact that a Latin American country was chosen as the site for the gathering. Colombia was originally designated as the host country, but the serious internal economic and social difficulties it was facing led the Colombian Government to refuse the nomination. Mexico was the next option.

The choice of a Latin American country is revealing. Where else, one might ask, could the Conference have been held? The United States would probably not have been a propitious choice—after all, the numerous and well-organized feminist movements there would have intervened to press their demands and might well have sabotaged or taken over the occasion. Also, an American venue would have amounted to an open admission of its hegemony; much better to demonstrate its 'neutrality' in the matter. Europe, the traditional seat of so many congresses, conferences and seminars of every variety, also has its fair share of politicized women's movements and overtly feminist tendencies; so there would have been little chance of establishing the sort of 'sisterhood' peddled in Mexico. The remaining alternative was what is called the 'Third World'. This had the advantage for the industrialized countries of providing them with an opportunity to illustrate, if only formally, the progress being made in these 'underdeveloped' countries, which are still being pillaged and exploited despite the rapid spread of revolutionary and nationalist ideas.

Within this 'Third World' itself, the choice was not difficult. The Arab countries with their sexist culture are still denying women any voice of their own, and were obviously out. In Asia, either famine and destitution prevail or else a revolutionary process is in full swing. Africa is impoverished, divided and politically unstable. Of the Latin American countries, one could discount those where revolutionary struggles are being waged despite the repression exercised by a well-equipped imperialism. Mexico was a natural choice. Despite its progressive image abroad, the country's domestic policy is based on the repression of opposition movements and tight control over trade union, peasant and professional organizations.

The World Conference on Women was a reformist and official gathering in which women were represented by a few 'distinguished ladies', usually the wives of Deputies or Ministers, and by women of the ruling class generally, rather than by working women.

The political presence of Latin American women is more and more making itself felt. Women of the exploited classes are increasingly organizing themselves and partic------ipating in popular movements. Petty-bourgeois women have established their own groups to defend their interests. The influence of the European and North American women's movements is growing. In the face of all this, governments are attempting to recuperate the movement, or rather to set up travestied versions of it which not only present no threat to the regime but may even be useful to it in some ways. But the regimes' efforts are mainly aimed at bourgeois or middle-class women, excluding the vast majority of women workers and peasants. The (at best) reformist nature of these 'official' movements means that they can never hope to resolve the problems of the exploited, especially those of oppressed women. In countries where it is still safe for the system to maintain apparently 'democratic' governments, as in Colombia, Venezuela and Mexico, women's votes help consolidate the image. For instance, the present President of Colombia came to power by giving his election campaign a distinctly feminist tone and responding positively to some of the demands of bourgeois and petty-bourgeois women, for instance on divorce.

It is in this context that one must understand the publicity campaigns launched by the Latin American governments and their haste to mobilize women. But the process did not develop spontaneously. It was triggered by the U.N. declaring 1975 International Women's Year and reached its bureaucratic climax with the World Conference in Mexico.

Notes

1. This section is obviously only an historical outline of women's participation in the social struggles which have characterized Latin American history right up to the present day. The almost total unavailability of information concerning many countries naturally means that it remains very limited and incomplete.
2. Fray Bartolomé de las Casas, a Spanish historian and missionary, in the 16th Century denounced the genocide practised against the Indians. His works form part of a body of texts which have come to be known as the *leyenda negra* (the black legend) in Spanish colonial historiography. Fray Bartolomé de las Casas, *Breve relato de la destrucción de las indias*, in A. Saint-lu, 'Las Casas et les femmes des conquistadores et des colons', *Caravelle*, Université de Toulouse, CMHLB, p. 191.
3. M. Hamerly, *Historia social y économica de la antigua provincia de Guayaquil, 1763–1842*, Guayaquil: 1973, pp. 156–7.
4. *Ibid.*, p. 158.
5. 'The Servant Problem', *Ellas*, No. 204, 31 August 1975, Caracas, Venezuela, p. 14.
6. Maria Antonieta Rascón, 'La Mujer y la Lucha Social', *Imagen y Realidad de la Mujer*, Mexico: 1975, Sepsetentas, No. 172, p. 139.
7. *Ibid.*, p. 140.
8. Choy Emilio, *Sobre la Revolución de Tupac Amaru*, Lima: Universidad Mayor de San Marcos, 1970, p. 17.
9. Paraguay, now decimated, passed a law authorizing polygamy, in order to increase the population more rapidly.
10. In 1817, in Brazil, there were 1,930,000 slaves and 585,000 free blacks out of a total population of 3,817,000 people. Cf. R. Bastide, *Les Ameriques noires*, Paris: 1967, Payot, p. 13.
11. *Jus Suffragi*, journal of the International Alliance for Women's Suffrage, No. 9, May 1914, p. 105.
12. Rascon, *op. cit.,* pp. 139–74.
13. A. Zendejas, 'Entretien avec Margarita Garcia Flores', *Fem*, Vol. 1, No. 1, Oct–Dec 1976, Mexico, pp. 68–76.
14. *Ibid.*, p. 70.

15. Rascon, *op. cit.,* p. 174.
16. *Nouvelles du Mexique*, No. 2, July 1955.
17. Isabel Pico Vidal, 'La mujer marginada por la historia', *El Mundo*, San Juan, Puerto Rico, 27 June 1975.
18. L. Capezzuoli and G. Cappabianca, *Historia de la emancipación femenina*, Buenos Aires: Ed. Futuro, 1966, p. 182.
19. *Ibid.*
20. M. Romano Yalour de Tobar, *Como educan los argentinos a sus hijos*, Buenos Aires: Ed. Libera, 1969, p. 20.
21. C., Grierson, *International Council of Women*, 2nd quinquennial meeting, London 1899, London: T. Fisher Unwin, 1900.
22. *International Council of Women*, Documents of the first two reports on the 7th quinquennial period, 1920–1922.
23. Celia La Palma de Emery, Honorary Inspector of Women and Children's Work, states that charity work is 'a living example of the constant and well-managed activity of the rich women of our country'. *Acción pública y privada en favor de la mujer y del niño*, Buenos Aires: 1910, p. 186.
24. Rascon, *op. cit.,* p. 155.
25. 'Report of the Constituent Congress' in Rascon, *op. cit.*, p. 157.
26. *Ibid.*
27. Zendejas, *op. cit.*, pp. 73–4.
28. *Ibid.*
29. It disappeared more or less at the same time as the independent workers movement and the student and youth movements. Cf. *Ibid.*, p. 72.
30. A women's suffrage movement.
31. See Torres Giraldo Ignacio, *Maria Cano, mujer rebelde*, Bogota: Ed. La Rosca, 1972.
32. See Pinzón Gómez Patricia, 'Compartamiento Político Femenino', (unpublished thesis), Bogota: Department of Political Science, Universidad de los Andes, 1972.
33. H. Saffioti, *A Mulher na Sociedada de Classes: Mito & Realidade*, Sao Paolo: Livraria Quarto Artes, 1969.
34. *Havana Journal of the Cuban Revolutionary Party* (CPP (A)), led by Andrés Grau San Martin, President of the Republic from 1944 to 1948, national-reformist tendency.
35. *Jus Suffragi*, No. 7, March 1914, p. 77.
36. Isabel Pico Vidal, *op. cit.*
37. *Ibid.*
38. Prospectus of the First Venezuelan Women's Congress, Caracas: 1974.
39. *Movimiento Hacia la Nueva Mujer*, Bulletin No. 2, Caracas: 1975.
40. (A. de) Josefina Almeida, *La Ley y el Status de la Mujer en Colombia*, Contribucion al Año Internacional de la Mujer, International Advisory Committee on Population and Law with the co-operation of Harvard and Tufts Universities, Medford, Mass.: 1975, p. 40.

41. See Ramon Ramirez, *El movimiento estudiantil de 1968*, Mexico: 1970; and Elena Poniatowsko, *La noche de Tlatelolco*, Mexico: ERA, 1969.
42. A recently published yearbook lists all the women's organizations in Mexico.
43. See *Fem*, Vol. 1, No. 1, Oct–Dec 1976, pp. 25, 76; and *Novedades*, 17 September 1976.
44. In Puerto Rico, girl-children are called *chancletas*, for their horizons should supposedly not go beyond the home, rather as slippers are house-shoes which no one would dream of wearing outside. Now the 'slippers' have grown heels and are ready to step out into the street, and into the social world at large.
45. M. Randall, 'La Mujer Cubana Ahora' quoted in Carlos Serrano, 'La Femme et le socialisme á Cuba', *Cuba-si* (Journal for the France-Cuba Association) No. 55, January 1976.
46. Jean Pierre Jasz, 'Fiche signalétique sur la Fédération des Femmes Cubaines', *Cuba-si*, No. 55, January 1976.

The 'Wages for Housework' Trap

In recent years, certain feminist currents in the developed countries, notably in Italy, Britain and the U.S., have demanded wages for housework. Starting from the assumption that all women are to some extent house-keepers, and that housework is productive labour, these groups have called on the state to pay a salary to all women involved in keeping a home. They claim that this demand is revolutionary in that, far from tying women to the home, it will destroy the traditional housewife's role. Pressing this demand, they argue, is effectively to attack the structure of the family and thereby threaten the very basis of capitalism.

The groups who support the 'wages for housework' campaign have tried to introduce the idea in Mexico and other Latin American countries without, however, taking account of the socio-economic context of the area in general or of the particular circumstances pertaining to each country within it. We want to show how this position represents merely another attempt to impose individualist demands from abroad (Italy, U.K., U.S.) which correspond neither to the needs nor to the experience of most Latin American women. The position is both reformist and economistic and fails to address the central issue of the reorganization of housework on a *social* basis. Nor does this approach resolve any of the other issues facing women, since it provides no realistic answer to the question of how society as a whole can be changed. We have used this debate as a detailed example illustrating the deviations which the women's movement may fall into if it loses sight of the fundamental issues and forgets that the overall aim is to break the basis and social structures of the capitalist system.

Domestic Labour

Before the capitalist system emerged, the patriarchal family fulfilled simultaneously various economic and social functions. It served as a centre of production in which every member participated in different capacities to ensure the survival of the family as a whole. There was already some division of labour according to sex,[1] but because women fulfilled an economic function, their work was recognized as useful and important for society. In this framework, there was no rigid separation of private and public activities. Then, as the nascent bourgeoisie gradually appropriated the means of production and the capitalist system developed, the family began to lose its productive function. A decisive break between the public sphere (the factory) and the private sphere (the home) was established. Women were confined to the world of the home and consequently excluded from all productive economic activity.[2]

From then on, economic, political and cultural changes in the public sphere determined the evolution of the old extended family into the present nuclear family characteristic of industrial societies. By reducing women to the role of housewives, the division of social life into two spheres has perpetuated the patriarchal family and has, amongst other effects, ensured women's total economic dependence upon men.

Within this new framework, women's main role in life has been to reproduce and service labour power. The specific activity of women 'considered in their role as wives and mothers' can thus be defined as 'those activities necessary to the reproduction of labour power in all its physical, psychological and ideological aspects; activities which are, amongst other things, unpaid, characterized by personal and affective bonds between the agents, and carried out in a private place which is apparently separate from the overall social process.'[3] Women's tasks have indeed been allocated them as activities to be carried out in the home, and are thus separate from the other activities involved in social reproduction, for instance those of the army, the schools, etc. However, they are not simply reducible to housework. Obviously housework is one component (cooking, cleaning, washing, etc.) but because it is socially useful, necessary and not implicitly personal it could be accomplished collectively and without discrimination by all members of the family or, better still, by society at large. Emotional and moral support, on the other hand, cannot be taken as simply another aspect of women's domestic activity. It corresponds to all the feelings and affective bonds which develop in an interpersonal relationship. Emotions are personal, and therefore not interchangeable; they cannot be quantified or defined in terms of economic relations of production, as housework can be. Nonetheless, because affective relations within the family are strongly influenced by the existing relations of production, they are used manipulatively, to justify the fact that housework is a role reserved for women; in this way they help to maintain the oppression women suffer.

The groups who support the 'wages for housework' campaign generally define housework as 'the material labour, sexual activities and emotional roles which are demanded of us and which we feel obliged to fulfil, since our ultimate function is to ensure the well-being of the "other" rather than our own.'[4]

In another article written in the U.S. and published by a British group, our role as women is described as that of unpaid but happy workers, 'loving servants of the working class'. Just as God created Eve to please Adam, so capital has created the housewife to serve the worker physically, emotionally and sexually, to bring up his children, mend his socks, and patch up his ego when he is depressed by the work and social relations assigned to him by capitalism. It is precisely this mixture of physical, emotional and sexual services demanded by capital of women which makes her work as servant-housewife so tiring yet so intangible.[5]

According to these definitions anything a woman does, including love and interpersonal relations, is work, and as work, it ought to be paid. But this view of traditionally female activities confuses work with affective relations and with the various forms of expression particular to women. To lump work, social relations, personal expression and 'domesticity' all together as aspects of 'female' servitude denies all creative potential to human relations and evacuates all meaning from the concept of work.

Housework, considered as a predominantly female
activity, is also defined in terms of the role played by
women in society: 'Women . . . have been isolated in the
home and forced to do what is considered unskilled work,
namely giving birth to the work force, bringing it up and
servicing it. Their role in the cycle of social production has
remained invisible because only the product of their
labour, *the worker*, was visible.'[6] According to the definition
presented by M. Dalla Costa and Selma James in their book
The Power of Women and the Subversion of the Community, what
women produce

> . . . is a strange kind of commodity because it is not a 'thing'.
> The ability to labour resides only in a human being whose life is
> consumed in the process of producing. First it must be nine
> months in the womb, must be fed, clothed and trained, then
> when it works, its beds must be made, its floors swept, its lunch
> box prepared, its sexuality not gratified but quietened . . . To
> describe its basic production and reproduction is to describe
> women's work.[7]

While this definition does not explicitly mention
emotional relations as an aspect of housework, it should be
remembered that the article was published in 1971, before
the wages for housework campaign really got off the
ground. The book served as the theoretical basis for all the
later developments, and in it housework is clearly defined
as productive labour: 'What we are trying to say is that
housework is productive labour in the Marxist sense of the
word; it is work which produces surplus value.'[8] Now, it is
certainly true that housework is essential to the production
of surplus value since it reproduces the labour power which
will in turn directly produce surplus value. But this work
does not itself *directly* produce surplus value, nor is it
exploited in a wage-labour relation. Housework cannot
therefore be considered as productive labour in the Marxist
sense of the term.

In the preface to the Latin American edition of the book,
the authors restate their definition of housework as
productive labour, and in so doing, manage to misquote
Marx:

This book attempts to demonstrate why there is such a great difference between the technique for extracting and refining oil and the technique for extracting and refining oil workers. We try to show that the oil worker's wife is as productive as he is since each and every day she 'directly produces, trains, develops, maintains and reproduces labour power itself'.[9]

Marx repeatedly gives precise definitions of productive labour:

> A singer who sings like a bird is not a productive worker; to the extent that she sells her song for money she is both a wage-earner and a merchant. But this same singer becomes a productive worker the moment she is hired by an entrepreneur to sing and make money, since she directly *produces* capital. A teacher in the schoolroom is not a productive worker; but he becomes productive when he is hired to realize the value invested by the owner of an establishment which sells knowledge....[10] ... a schoolmaster is a productive worker when, in addition to working in order to improve the intelligence of his scholars, he slaves to enrich the school proprietor.[11]

So teachers are not productive just because they 'form the minds' of their pupils, even though by doing so they contribute to the replenishment of labour power since their pupils will eventually become workers employed by capital. Teachers are only productive when they add value to the capital invested by the owner of the school. Similarly, those people whose domestic labour reproduces and maintains labour power cannot be considered as productive workers either.

To sum up, housework is a set of material, impersonal and interchangeable activities carried out within the family nexus almost exclusively by women. The social function of this housework is to reproduce and maintain the labour force, but that in itself does not qualify it as productive labour in the Marxist sense of the term.

Wages for Housework

There is nothing new about the present wages for
housework campaign conducted by certain feminist groups.
The problem of assessing housework in financial terms was
raised as early as 1878 in an International Women's
Congress attended by feminists from twenty-seven different
countries, including Brazil. One of the proposals presented
then was that housework should be considered equivalent
to paid work done by men. Nearly a century later, certain
women's groups are once again announcing the need to
fight for housework to be recognized as productive labour
which ought to be paid for by the state.

These groups originally emerged in Britain, Italy and the
U.S., and attempted to develop support for their ideas, first
in the other industrialized countries, then throughout the
world. They have presented their struggle as a universal
one, since all women are 'domestic workers' and since 'it is
precisely what is particular to housework . . . which determines a woman's place, wherever she is and to whichever class
she belongs.'[12]

In the industrialized countries where the demand was
first put forward, development has made it possible for
women to be incorporated into the industrial and tertiary
sector labour markets. Female labour power in these
countries has historically been mobilized *en masse* during
periods of war economy, then forced back into the confines
of the family and housework during the periodic crises of
capitalism. In post-war periods, women's expulsion from
the labour market has been determined by the return of
the men to their old jobs and by the exigencies of
reproducing the labour force and expanding the population,
in order to rebuild the country and stimulate production.

The relatively large and powerful feminist movements in
Western Europe and the U.S. need to reach an
increasingly large number of women if they are to continue
growing. Generally speaking, a majority of women in these
countries are housewives who, because of their isolated
working conditions, have been particularly resistant to the
efforts of the feminist movement. This is one reason why
certain groups have sought to develop a campaign aimed
specifically at housewives as part of a commitment to

reaching a larger number of women of all social classes.

The present economic crisis in the capitalist countries has now spread to the rest of the world. As on previous occasions it has led to a contraction of the labour market, a circumstance in which women are always the first to be fired or refused work. This is partly due to the insecurity and precariousness of women's employment, but also because it is often true that women's salaries are not absolutely essential to the family budget. Women's unemployment is not taken seriously because it is felt that they can always go back to their 'natural' occupation, namely housework. At times like these, governments use all sorts of 'economic', 'sociological' and 'psychological' arguments to convince women of the importance of staying at home and carrying out the duties of a wife and mother.

In the countries most affected by the present crisis (Britain, Italy), the way was thus left wide open for certain feminist groups to raise the issue of wages for housework. The demand came precisely at the moment when the European governments were seeking to reduce the unemployment problem by forcing women workers back into the home, a measure which has the added advantage of reinforcing family structures and the capitalist system.

Within the capitalist system, the female labour force is seen as an important part of the reserve army of labour. During *man*power shortages, this army is mobilized, only to be thrown back into the family during economic crises and periods when the labour market is contracting. The unemployed and, in the industrialized countries, the surplus manpower in the so-called less developed regions also form part of this reserve army.

Even so, this is no reason to argue, as some authors have done, that immigration and the importation of foreign labour constitute a new strategy aimed at keeping women out of the production process. Under the capitalist system, the factor which determines the incorporation of labour in the economic cycle is the cost of production and reproduction. In the case of immigrants, the host state does not have to cover these costs. Furthermore, the salaries and working conditions imposed on immigrant workers tend to be unacceptable to local workers, including even the women.[13]

In order to incorporate women massively into the labour market, one would have both to improve these conditions and provide extensive collective social services which would reduce the present burden of housework (creches, canteens, public laundries, etc.). It is this combination of costs which capital, and hence capitalist governments, will bear in mind if they are ever faced with the choice of either incorporating women into the labour market or keeping them at home by paying wages for housework.

The Trap

The feminist groups at the forefront of the wages for housework struggle present their demands as a common aim which can unite all women and destroy the housewife's role. The monotonous, boring and stupefying activities which account for the greater part of housework and which limit women's creativity would at last be paid for and, even more important, recognized as work. Housework would then no longer be considered as a task which 'naturally' falls to women. Wages for housework would supposedly also represent a break with the idea that women are (must be) the source of a family's peace and well-being thanks to their traditionally 'feminine' qualities. These are the reasons for which it is claimed that 'wages for housework' would destroy the structures of the family and hence the very basis of the capitalist system.

Furthermore, it is repeatedly stated that women would not necessarily be the ones to do the housework if wages were available for it: 'Our needs and desires are international— to be free from the work which has kept us subordinate for centuries, to be free from domination by and dependence on men ... What we need is a wage, not the work.'[14]

But these wages would not really be wages. They would be more akin to an unearned income, since there would be no guarantee of output in exchange. What would these wages without work represent? The possibility of being free and independent (so the answer goes), the possibility of 'leaving the house, not to take up another job but to join a strike picket'.[15] Just how utopian can you get? The suggestion here is that the state is going to pay women a wage so that they can 'freely and independently' engage full-time in activities aimed at destroying the state itself. Apart from its obvious unlikelihood, it is difficult to see how the necessary massive mobilization of housewives could ever be effected and organized, given the strength of the emotional bonds between women, children and men.

What would be the real effect of wages for housework? We believe it would in fact lead to the institutionalization of a division of labour based on sex and to a permanent discrimination against women. Instead of stimulating change, such a measure would strengthen the traditional system of male-female relations, the structures of the patriarchal family and hence the capitalist system. It is not impossible that male demands on women could actually increase as a result—housework would be treated as 'women's work', and since women would be paid for doing it, men would expect them to put even more effort into it.

These wages would thus constitute one more mechanism by which women could be kept in the home, denied access to other types of work, and prevented from developing their personality outside the narrow confines of the home. Of course, we believe in the struggle to stop housework being a form of slavery and domination. We accept that it should be considered as work (according to our definition) and not as a characteristic and natural occupation of women. However, the idea that demanding wages for housework is going to achieve all this is completely wrong. If these wages were ever paid, they would accentuate the commercialization of human relationships in society as a whole, since this commercialization would be implanted quite explicitly within the family itself. By extension, all personal relations would become functions of the economic system, a grotesque reproduction of the dominant social relations under capitalism.

Up till now, housework has functioned as a means of excluding women from social, political and economic activity. Since this work is in itself useful and necessary to society as a whole, it ought to be carried out in such a way that it is not made a site of discrimination and exploitation. In other words, it must be separated from the family context and undertaken by society at large, by men and women, without discrimination.

Notes

1. F. Engels, *The Origin of the Family, Private Property and the State*, various eds.
2. Isabel Larguia and John Dumoulin, *Hacia una Ciencia de la Liberacion de la Mujer*, Havana: Casa de Las Americas, Nos. 65–66, 1971.
3. Robert Leparc, 'Capitalisme et Patriarcat à travers l'Analyse Economique du Travail Feminin', *Critiques de l'Economie Politique*, Nos. 11–12, April–September 1973, p. 184 (our italics).
4. Marina Zancan, *Salario para el Trabajo Doméstico*, Comité de Mestre Venezia, Lotta Feminista, 1975.
5. Silva Federici, *Wages Against Housework*, London: Power of Women Collective and Falling Wall Press, 1975, p. 3.
6. Mariarosa Dalla Costa and Selma James, *The Power of Women and the Subversion of the Community*, London: Power of Women Collective and Falling Wall Press, 1975, p. 28.
7. *Ibid.*, p. 11ff.
8. *Ibid.*
9. Selma James, 'All Work and No Pay', *Women, Housework and the Wages Due*, London: Power of Women Collective and the Falling Wall Press, 1975, p. 25ff. In defining productive labour, Selma James refers to Marx's *Theories of Surplus Value*, Part One, London: Lawrence and Wishart, 1969, p. 172: 'Productive labour would *therefore* be such labour as produces commodities or directly produces, trains, develops, maintains *or* reproduces labour power itself.' But in fact Marx is clearly analyzing Adam Smith's definition of productive labour rather than providing his own. The very next sentence continues: 'Adam Smith excludes the latter from his category of productive labour—arbitrarily but with a certain correct instinct that, if he included it, this would open the floodgates for false pretensions to the title of productive labour.'
10. Karl Marx, *Un Chapitre Inedit du Capital*, coll. 10/18, Paris: 1971, p. 233.
11. Karl Marx, *Capital*, Vol II, Book I, London: Lawrence and Wishart (our italics).
12. Dalla Costa and James, *op. cit.*, p. 21.
13. Leparc, *op. cit.,* p. 181.
14. James, *op. cit.*, p. 13.
15. Dalla Costa and James, *op. cit.*, p. 15.

Part Two

Guadeloupe and Martinique: Ethnocide and Traditional Employment

Until 1848, the Antilles (Martinique and Guadeloupe) were slave colonies. But the abolition of slavery, brought about mainly as a result of the struggles of the slaves themselves, did little to change the colonial status of the Antilles. In 1946, the Antilles became a French *Departement*. This judicial sleight of hand in no way altered our countries' dependence upon France. Our countries were kept in a state of economic, political and cultural subordination solely in the interests of the French bourgeoisie and its local allies. After thirty years of '*Departementalization*', the economic and social situation is steadily getting worse. Agriculture, the only activity developed by French colonialism, continues to regress. The workers' standard of living is falling lower and lower. Two out of every three workers are unemployed, the cost of living is very high and the official rate of inflation is 23 per cent.[1]

Women's Employment

Women in the Antilles are exposed to the super-exploitation and oppression which is the lot of all women under the capitalist system, but their condition is made worse by the fact that they are also colonized women. The structure of the family, low wages, endemic unemployment and under-employment force women to take on work wherever possible. Forty per cent of women are economically active, and suffer a specific kind of super-exploitation. In the Antilles, unemployment is an essential feature of the social situation, with 60 per cent of the active population completely or partly unemployed.[2] Women are particularly affected; according to official sources 35 per cent of them are completely unemployed, as against 20 per cent for the men. The modernization of the sectors in which women have traditionally been employed (agriculture, shopkeeping) has made matters worse.

Women constitute a pool of largely unskilled labour which serves the interests of capital. Because of the shortage of jobs due to colonial underdevelopment, they are prepared to accept the worst possible wages and working conditions. This job situation makes possible all sorts of pressures: employment contracts are rare, job security non-existent. Women in the Antilles usually end up in declining economic sectors where they are given the most unpleasant or unskilled jobs.

Employment of Women

Retail Trade	9%
Agricultural Work	11%
Domestic Service	25%

They get very low wages, even for *Departements* where the guaranteed minimum wage is 35 per cent lower than in other French *Departements* and even though the cost of living in the Antilles is higher. (State employees are given a 40 per cent cost of living allowance.) More than half of the working women get wages lower than the local miminum wage (about 800 francs a month). A servant who works more than eight hours a day, six days a week, gets only 300 to 400 francs a month.

The kind of training available to women tends to reinforce the system. For instance, the Pilote River job training centre in Martinique was set up to 'train domestic staff in the countryside'. But many women admit they attend the centre merely to get a few months' guaranteed wages.

To manage the difficult economic situation in the Antilles, the French Government has come up with two solutions: emigration and birth control. In order to promote emigration, it set up in 1963 the 'Bureau pour le development des migrations interessant les departements d'outre-mer' (B.U.M.I.D.O.M., the Office for the Promotion of Migration from the Overseas *Departements*). Emigrant women often spend some time at the B.U.M.I.D.O.M. training centre at Crouy-sur-Ourq, where they are taught 'discipline, hygiene and the use of the domestic appliances they will be provided with by their employers in the city'. Those who look for a job on their own initiative usually end up, like most workers from the Antilles, in the worst public sector jobs: they become Post Office auxiliaries, hospital cleaners or servants. They are also the first to be fired. The case of Mme X, who worked for ten years as a social worker, was refused a regular post and then fired for supposed incompetence, is fairly typical.

The government is also promoting birth control. Contraception is used as an instrument of economic policy. Sterilization is the most common method. Family allowances are also used as an incentive to reduce the birth rate—the state contributes progressively less for the upkeep of a third or subsequent child. To take an example, Mme T is a servant, who has twelve children, none of whom work. She gets 958 francs to feed and clothe thirteen people. Women are thus forced to take on several jobs to supplement their income.

The Family

Ideological oppression is ubiquitous, manifesting itself through the family, education, assimilationist ideas and *machismo*. The family structure of the contemporary Antilles is an inheritance from the days of the slave trade, when it was quite impossible to create a stable family system. Marriage is still uncommon amongst the poor; only 30 per cent of women are married and 50 per cent of children are 'illegitimate', even though marriage is the ideal set up by the colonizers. Women hope that their daughters will marry and thereby improve their social status, especially if they themselves are not married. They bring up their sons and daughters differently, teaching the girls to serve their masters, the men. Mothers generally hope to have sons, rather than daughters for whom they will have to try to find a husband.

The family is the main nexus in which the ideological superstructure is articulated with the colonial economic structure, and in many families, girls are taught to despise their own culture.

Education

Schooling is organized on the same lines as in France, with little attention paid to local culture, and no official recognition of the possibility of teaching Creole. 'Although Creole is the mother tongue of practically the entire population of Haiti, the Antilles and French Guyana, and although it remains the most common language in the islands, it is generally treated as a pidgin language which people are ashamed to speak.' . . . 'speaking French is a sign of wealth and is thus seen as desirable by those who aspire to a better life.'[3]

The education system is currently reinforcing women's inequality by adapting the female labour force to the needs of the colonialists. Girls often go straight into work from primary school, while in the technical colleges, girls are pushed towards the tertiary sector where they will work as typists, office clerks or secretaries.

The Church also plays an important role in the Antilles, where most people are practising Christians, whose religion counsels fatalistic resignation, especially to women.

Sexual Oppression

Women in the Antilles are also exposed to *machismo* exacerbated sexual oppression, compounded by certain features specific to colonization. In the days of the slave trade it was the white *colon* (settler) who occupied the *macho* role. His slaves were at his disposal in every way, including sexually. This ideology has now spread throughout Antilles society. Making love is considered reprehensible for a woman; a woman who is sexually free will be treated as a whore, although a man's sexual exploits will be taken as signs of virility and status. Amongst the poorer strata of society, relationships are unstable and the women often end up abandoned. A woman has a child and is then deserted; she moves in with another man, has a second child and is deserted again; and so on. The many illegitimate children in the Antilles are a blatant indication of the social irresponsibility of the men.

Even amongst the petty bourgeoisie, where women face different problems, they suffer the effects of *machismo*. They have to take complete responsibility for the home (children, the family housekeeping, etc.), while the men go out with their friends and mistresses; if the woman is unmarried, her situation is even worse.

Ethnocide

The concept of ethnocide, as developed by Pierre Clastres amongst others, is exemplified in the Antilles. Clastres contrasts it with genocide and gives the following definition: 'While the term "genocide" refers to an idea of "race" and to a desire to exterminate a racial minority, "ethnocide" indicates an attempt to destroy a people's culture. Genocide murders people physically, ethnocide kills their spirit.'[4]

In the Antilles, this kind of depersonalization is evident in extreme forms of denigration of local values and national identity. Assimilation of Western values is presented as the universal ideal. Women from Guadeloupe and Martinique actually 'disguise' themselves as women from Guadeloupe and Martinique; they dress up in their own costumes rather as one might dress up as a 'dancer' or a 'gypsy'. The press and fashion promote assimilation by emphasizing certain resemblances between the oppressed and the oppressor, whose real features are thus hidden behind the same uniform mask. It is just another way of denying that women from the Antilles are different from French women and have an identity of their own.

The so-called 'women's' magazines such as *Intimite, Marie Claire*, etc. play a considerable role in this process. They help confine women to the 'feminine' realms and offer endless prescriptions indicating the proper bourgeois way of doing everything and anything, from preparing a meal to conducting an affair. Even if we recognize that women in the Antilles are to some extent searching for their own identity through hairstyles, dress, etc., they make no attempt to question the position they occupy in colonial society.

Obviously all this is only one approach to the experience of women in the Antilles. Women there have not yet begun to deal with their particular problems. Autonomous and class-based organization is still very much in its infancy.

Notes

1. In France, the inflation rate reached 11.8 per cent in 1975 (see *Atlaseco, Nouvel Observateur*, 1976).
2. In France the rate of unemployment was about 4 per cent in 1976 (see *Le Monde*, 8 March 1977).
3. J. Collard, 'Une langue non écrite: Quel avenir le créole?', *Le Monde*, 26 January 1977.
4. Pierre Clastres, 'De l'ethnocide', *Encyclopaedia Universalis*, published in *L'Homme*, Vol. XIV, No. 34, July–December, 1974, pp. 101–110.

Bolivia: Women and the Class Struggle

This is the account of a trade union leader who, from her youth, has fought with exemplary valour and tenacity, alongside the exploited classes, to reclaim her people's democratic rights. Like many other women, she has suffered persecution, prison and exile as a result. Despite material difficulties and failing health, she continues her struggle with admirable courage and generosity.

The problem of women cannot be considered separately from its context within the class struggle. Like all social phenomena, its basis lies in historical conditions linked to the process of production and distribution.

Bolivia is primarily a country under the sway of world capitalism. But whereas capitalism has introduced very advanced techniques in the sectors concerned with the extraction of certain important raw materials, in other sectors of the economy the old forms of exploitation still persist.

Women began to be integrated into the process of production from 1900 onwards, when Bolivia was first exposed to the effects of penetration by big finance capital. But it was mainly women in the cities who competed with the men in keeping up with the brutalizing rhythm set by the new machines. In the feudal countryside, both men and women carried on with the old forms of production, ploughing the fields, sowing, harvesting and transporting the crops, without drawing any demarcation lines between their various tasks. Peasant women would gather in the crop—maize, wheat, beans or potatoes—load the heaviest sacks on the back of an animal and skilfully secure them with leather straps. Then they would take what was left on their own backs and set off, carrying their burden for miles if necessary.

Meanwhile, in the towns, women who once worked as artisans, often in small home-based workshops, now had to make their way to the factory.

Down the Mine

The Bolivian economy is mainly (86 per cent) based on the extraction of minerals, especially tin. This has produced a society in which different levels of historical development co-exist and constantly adjust to each other. A tiny layer of Bolivian society has acquired such political and economic importance that it is the centre of gravity of the entire life of the nation. Yet the Bolivian proletariat is one of the worst paid in South America. The average life expectancy is twenty-six years; 26 per cent of the miners have silicosis; and Chagas disease, a malady typically associated with poverty, incapacitates 83 per cent of the population in the tropical areas of the country, according to World Health Organization statistics.[1] Apart from the sub-human conditions in the mines, the very fact of living permanently at an altitude of over 3,000 metres, in rarefied air, amounts to a flouting of the rules of biology. In this dramatic setting, women stoically share in the daily confrontation with the problems of economic production and the reproduction of life. The way politics has developed in Bolivia has had its effect on the miner's wife, so that the companion and mate who looks after the family budget is also a comrade in trade union and political struggles. She has had to learn to light fires on floors of beaten earth, and to carry water for miles, after seeking out one of the few and frequently *copagire*-polluted wells.[2] Along with her proletarian sister, the *palliri*, she has already acquired a high level of political consciousness, partly through the efforts of the well-developed political organizations of the mining proletariat.

Around the pit shafts, amidst the mountains of low grade ore extracted from the mines, the *palliris* can be seen chipping at the earth with small picks or tearing at it with their nails. '*Palliri*' means 'collector' in Quechua: all day long, these women skilfully sort through the crushed stones and fill their sacks with fragments of ore. They work with their babies on their backs, sometimes in the pouring rain, sometimes under the glaring heat of the sun. No social laws protect them, nor is there any legal limit to their working day. If they are lucky, their reward is a few loaves of bread and some coffee with which to restore their own strength and their children, many of whom accompany them to the pit head. Yet the *palliris* are amongst the most committed militants in Bolivian political and trade union struggles.

In the Countryside

On 9 April 1952 the peasant and working-class masses launched a revolution which was then usurped and betrayed by a petty-bourgeois party, the National Revolutionary Movement (M.N.R.). The country was delivered back into the hands of the imperialists and, although some changes were effected in the countryside, the 1953 agrarian reform did little to infuse the relations of production with any dynamism.

Some of the *gamonales*,[3] the big feudal landlords, have been replaced by political *caciques*[4] and small landowners. But the landless peasants remain under the domination of landlords, great or small, as do the seasonal workers who move constantly from one part of the country to another. Many of these seasonal workers are women. They can be seen working in the co-operatives and plantations of the *Yungas*[5] and around *Caranavi*,[6] bringing in the rice, cocoa and coffee crops before returning to their communities in the high plateaux or around the mines the moment the harvest is finished. This yearly migration has many repercussions on these communities, so many of whose people have to tear themselves away from their homes. One effect is constant interruption of their children's schooling.

In the Towns

It is, amongst others, these increasingly impoverished peasant families who are drawn to the towns by the prospect of factory work. However, national industry is still so recently established that it can absorb only a tiny

proportion of this labour force. The rest remain
unemployed, swelling the miserable ranks of the part-time
salesmen and artisans who congregate around the cities.
The population of the Bolivian towns also includes a
stratum of women who have found work in the retail trade.
Half housewife and half worker, they are forced to leave
their domestic tasks and their children in order to
supplement the income provided by husbands who work as
artisans or factory hands. Along with the washerwomen,
office staff, servants, secretaries, seamstresses and stall-
holders, these women form a vast stratum of people who
have often given courageous support to revolutionary
political movements.

It is worth mentioning that, in the middle classes, 50 per
cent of teachers are women. They get the same wages as
men and have repeatedly demonstrated their combativity in
wage demands. The teachers' trade union has been
affiliated to the Bolivian Workers Congress (C.O.B.) ever
since it was set up in April 1952 and has consistently
followed the line laid down by the fourth C.O.B.
conference in 1970. Furthermore, in 1971, the teachers
joined the workers in founding a Popular Assembly.
Successive Bolivian governments have learnt to fear the
combativity of the women teachers who are always amongst
the first to take to the streets and brave the police, the
dogs and the tear gas. Since August 1971 the fascist Banzer
regime has been taking particularly violent steps against
the unions. At the moment, teachers account for the
highest percentage of imprisoned women; the fascist
regime has even denied them the right to work while
behind bars.

In the Revolutionary Struggle

Ever since 1965, following the confrontation between the
proletariat and General Barrientos' dictatorship, trade
union leaders have been persecuted and assassinated during
revolts against a 40 per cent reduction in wages. As during
previous periods in Bolivia's dramatic political history,
concentration camps were set up in the inhospitable heart
of the Amazon forest. Around Christmas 1965, miners'

wives and women from the towns launched a hunger strike and demanded the return of the prisoners. The strike became a national issue and violence soon ensued. The government attacked the strikers with tear gas and sent in *agents provocateurs*, but the women held on and, ten days later, obtained the release of all the prisoners. Then in 1972, for the first time in the history of Latin America, a concentration camp exclusively for women was set up a few kilometres outside La Paz.

Today, women continue to fight within the various trade unions and often lead the struggle themselves. One example was the 1974 teachers' strike, which aroused the whole country. The Bolivian housewife keeps a close watch on the conditions imposed on her sisters in the prisons, providing moral and physical support.[7]

Last year, during the celebration of International Women's Year, the 'distinguished ladies' who were sent as official delegates to the world conference in Mexico did their best to ignore the fate of the majority of Bolivian women. But through their trade unions and workers' parties, the exploited women of Bolivia were able to refute the government's claim that working conditions are improving. The women of Bolivia know that one cannot avert one's eyes from misery, hunger, disease and illiteracy.

Notes

1. Chagas disease is a tropical illness transmitted by mosquitoes. The disease progresses slowly but is eventually fatal when, having affected the joints, it reaches the heart.
2. A mineral residue which contaminates rivers which are often the peasants' only source of water.
3. The traditional feudal owners of the latifundia, who still exercise great power over the peasants.
4. Peasant leaders who became bureaucratized following the agrarian reform.
5. A very hot valley region in the Andes.
6. The capital of a Bolivian province in the Yungas region to the north-east of La Paz which has a large peasant population and where many agricultural products are bought and sold (coffee, bananas, rice, quinine, coca, cocoa).
7. Some of them are even imprisoned outside the country. One young leader of the teachers' trade union is being held in Punta Arenas (Chile), one of Pinochet's prisons.

Chile: From Liberation to Manipulation

Women of Chile: A Short History

This text was contributed by the Comité Femmes Chili à Paris

The arrival of the Spanish in the 16th Century spelt ruin
for the social systems of Chile's indigenous population.
Although we cannot go into details about these local
institutions, it is worth pointing out that the old
matriarchal system, in which women held many special
privileges, still enjoyed great prestige in these neolithic or
post-neolithic societies. In such a vast territory, there were,
of course, regional variations.

The brutal imposition of a different economic order,
namely, a mode of production based on profit, disrupted all
human relations and interrupted the autonomous evolution
of the local culture. The status of women was as a result
profoundly altered. They lost the privileged position they
had held in the old community and were reduced to the
status of beasts of burden. Disappointed in their hopes of
instant wealth, the Spanish turned on the indigenous
population, both men and women, and forced them to
work to the point of exhaustion. From sunrise to sunset, in
the middle of winter when the water level was rising, they
were made to sift grains of gold from the river sand. The
women were put to work standing thigh deep in the
freezing water, their state of health, their aching backs and
their cries of pain quite immaterial to their new masters.
Women and children were sent down the mines to dig out
minerals alongside the men. The guards had whips and dogs
to enforce their authority. If a woman attempted to escape,

the Spaniards would cut off her breasts, as an example to the others.

In 1524, the Council of the Indies authorized slavery. In any case the invaders had not waited for such royal permission before enslaving their prisoners. Christians had no objection in principle to slavery, as long as those enslaved were Muslims or non-Catholics. Indigenous women were sold as slaves or as bond servants from the earliest days of the Conquest right up until the beginning of the War of Independence.

In the 17th Century, the unprofitable exploitation of the gold and silver mines was abandoned and the ruling class turned to agriculture and stockbreeding: the wheat and vines brought from Europe produced results beyond expectation. Domestic animals, especially cows, were now ranched on a massive scale, providing huge fortunes for the owners of the previously run-down latifundia. These developments brought some slight improvements to the condition of women, but women's role in the process of production had now been reduced to giving birth to the labour force required for the latifundia. Occasionally, they would be offered seasonal work, but the rest of their time was spent on domestic chores in a sordid hut, with no light, no furniture, no drinking water and no bed to sleep on.

The women of the bourgeoisie, freed by an army of servants from all domestic cares, dedicated themselves to cultivating the essentially 'feminine' virtues, as laid down by Hispanic tradition: gentleness, charm, piety and devotion to one's children. Politics, the liberal professions, business and management were all the exclusive preserve of their protectors, those superior beings, the men. These mythical images propagated by the dominant classes and the clergy eventually rooted themselves in the mentality of the petty bourgeoisie and even in popular culture. Later, after the industrial revolution, the dominant class was able to use increasingly technical means to transmit these false values and to impose a final and complete alienation upon women—or so it seemed.

As industry and trade developed, new managers, clerks and skilled workers were required, as well as more teachers and professionally trained people. University and secondary education boomed, especially towards the end of the 19th Century. A law was passed allowing women to attend the

University. Very few women actually registered at first, about two a year on average, and even they were considered almost scandalously daring. The new students all came from the middle classes, since the daughters of the big landowners would not have dreamt of giving up their duties as fashionable ladies just to imitate men. But higher education did enable a privileged few to exercise a profession and to enjoy real economic independence. It also led some of them to get involved in trade union issues, to become active in the political parties and even eventually to sit on the benches of Parliament.

This new emancipation of bourgeois women was only possible thanks to the exploitation of working-class women who worked as full-time servants in their families. A working-class man did not and still does not have the means to send his children to college. As for University, it has always been out of the question for the vast majority of boys and girls, most of whom still have to leave school before the end of their primary education.

In the early 20th Century, many ex-peasants and their families left the countryside and came to work in the nitrate mines. But they soon rebelled against the foreign industrialists, and were supported by their wives, who had suffered the same abominable exploitation. These women helped to organize the strikes and encouraged those who were frightened of confrontation. Indeed, in the many massacres which have punctuated Chile's brutal history of class struggle, hundreds of women have fallen alongside their sons and husbands, pierced by the bullets of the 'forces of law and order'.

In the '20s and '30s, echoes of the Russian Revolution sounded in the miners' camps. The dispossessed began to agitate, organize and rebel. Frightened, the bourgeoisie made a few concessions, such as a day off (unpaid) on Sunday. It cost them little to quieten the mood of unrest and safeguard their interests and principles. Even so, many industrialists completely disregarded the new laws, and agitation continued. The inspiration of the Russian people's seizure of power, clandestine reading of Marx and the atrocious level of exploitation together engendered a strong workers' organization in which the miners' wives participated actively.

But aside from the miners' camps, the peri-urban slums and the countryside, women were for the most part isolated in the home, cut off from any workers' organization. Their work was entirely domestic. Without any awareness of their own class interests, they did not doubt the validity of the myths imposed by the bourgeoisie: women were there to have children, their duties were entirely to their family and party politics were none of their business.

In the late '30s and '40s, private industry began to expand, especially textiles, canning and clothing. Ten per cent of the economically active female population—the country's reservoir of cheap labour—found employment in the factories. By 1970 20 per cent of working women were factory workers, 40 per cent were servants and 25 per cent worked as clerks for the government or the private sector. And of course these women carried on fulfilling their primary role as wives and mothers.

In 1970, the hopes of the masses soared. Disappointed by the failures of the Frei regime, working-class women gave their backing to Allende, whose programme included equal wages for equal work, rapid construction of nursery schools, free health care, a 100 per cent increase in family allowances and the installation of creches in factories. These promises were kept. During the three years of the Popular Unity Government, women and children were the main priority in matters of health and education. Many women who had never before participated in politics joined in the struggle for national liberation and the repossession of the country's natural wealth. And, of course, some Chilean women have always been aware that their own emancipation was closely linked to the country's economic independence and to the liberation of their class.

The bourgeoisie was quick to exploit the liberties they had acquired whilst in power and which Salvador Allende had promised not to undermine. Their aim was to provoke a crisis which would destroy Popular Chile. Abroad, the U.S. blocked all credits. At home, the bourgeoisie took advantage of the options available in a liberal democracy. The *hacendados* (big landowners) neither sowed nor harvested any crops, and they sent their herds to Argentina. The retailers and the bourgeoisie hoarded tons of non-perishable goods—their attics and cellars were soon full to bursting. As a result, all the problems of a black market were added to those caused by mismanaged production, blocked credits and the lack of exchange controls.

With C.I.A. financial backing, the Right was able to increase its communication resources, and to use the freedom of expression guaranteed by a liberal democracy. The opposition radio stations constantly attacked the government, claiming it to be incapable of ensuring supplies, and forecast massive shortages and even famine. When Fidel Castro came from Cuba, the television and radio stations clamoured endlessly that 'the tyrant of the Caribbean has come to steal the bread from the mouths of your children'. Non-politicized women, especially those stuck at home, were easy targets for the daily bombardment from the broadcasting services. When many vital products became scarce or disappeared altogether—one had to queue for hours to get soap, matches, oil, coffee, and sometimes even bread—women turned all too willingly to the radio commentators for information, unable to distinguish between the real and apparent causes of the shortages.

In January 1973, the leaders of the ruling class began to use their own women in active counter-revolutionary moves. The dominant ideology had already established a certain conception of 'femininity' as part of the 'natural' order of things. The stereotype was lightly retouched, but only marginally, since the bourgeoisie had no intention of upsetting its own social hierarchy. The Right now projected women as 'she-wolves' 'defending the interests of their home and families' against the Marxist onslaught. They took to the streets in mass demonstrations.

On 11 September 1973, the 'Chilean Road to Socialism' gave way to one of the most bloody dictatorships in the history of Latin America. The bourgeoisie and those women who had become alienated had contributed to the downfall of a popular government which had failed to protect itself adequately against the inevitable counter-revolutionary backlash.

Chilean Women and the Pinochet Dictatorship

This text has also been produced with the help of the Comité Femmes Chili.

The 11 September 1973 coup d'etat which overthrew Salvador Allende's Government caused a generalized crisis in the social structures of Chile. How did the crisis affect the role of women and how does the present military regime strive to give women a false identity? Women's role in society has been one of the weapons most effectively utilized by the regime in its official declarations and propaganda. The Junta has addressed itself very specifically to women in the hope of building up a social base for their economic and political projects by exalting 'feminine virtues'. In early 1974, the Junta even floated the idea of a monument to 'Chilean Womanhood'.

Under cover of rebuilding the bourgeois social order, the military have in reality set the whole Chilean social process back several decades, and have thereby blocked the development of women into free social beings in their own right. The Junta has also tried to stamp out the concept of class struggle by erecting an ideological screen to hide the real character of Chilean society. What the military regime is attempting is to restructure society according to 'biological' criteria such as age, sex, etc. In an interview published in the August 1975 issue of the magazine *Ecrilla*, Augusto Pinochet declared that: 'the more a woman is feminine, the more she is admirable . . . There is a natural and necessary complementarity between human beings. The sexes are not competitors, they complement each other. Women deserve our affection and respect. Nobody should ever forget that they are born of a woman, their mother.'

In the traditional schema of bourgeois ideology, women are the cornerstone of the social edifice. The Chilean military regime has every reason to reinforce this traditional conception of women, who can then be cast as symbols of the nation and the guardians of morality. Women's part in the bourgeoisie's counter-revolutionary manoeuvres against the Popular Unity Government in December 1971 and after was presented as 'a sacred struggle to preserve the identity of women and society as a whole'.

75

In March 1976, the Rector of the University of Chile, Colonel Julio Tapia, outlined the Junta's viewpoint as follows: 'We Chileans are well placed to assess the role that women have played and still play in the progress of contemporary society. I would even go so far as to say that throughout the history of our nation, Chilean women, *our women*, have manifested not only great intelligence and emotional strength but also an ability and nobility which have made them the driving force of our nationalism.' It would be interesting to see precisely which women are being referred to as 'our women', given that the traditional feminine image which corresponds to 'his' women can only be maintained by the women of the upper classes and not by the exploited sectors who today face increasing poverty and repression. But it is identifications such as this which enable the regime to persecute those women who do not accept the traditional model and who struggle for social change. Dissident women in Chile have nothing in common with the military's stereotype of a delicate, sensitive femininity which turns women into a prop for reaction.

The women who oppose the Junta's tyranny soon discover that 'femininity' is no protection against rape and torture. It is the treatment reserved for dissident and politically committed women which finally underlines the regime's profoundly machist criteria. The moment a woman becomes a political person, she immediately loses any claim on the respect supposedly owed to her in the role as wife and mother. Whatever her social origins, she becomes the butt of the most vulgar sarcasms and contempt. Other actions demonstrate the regime's ideological line, from the ban on women wearing 'anti-feminine' garments such as trousers[1] (the law has since been repealed) to the sexual violence exercised against women dissidents.

According to the present Chilean Government, feminist struggles waged in other countries to solve the problems peculiar to women take them away from their 'fundamental role'. In a tribute to Chilean womanhood organized by the Rotary Club, its President declared:

> Throughout the world, we have sought to stress the primordial role of women in the family, the home and in society at large. All the communities which form a nation

find the essential inspiration of their activity and their
spiritual development in their women . . . . Chilean women,
with the characteristic wisdom and profundity we all respect
so much, have understood that their task is to build a solid
united nation infused with a great ideal of solidarity. Unlike
some women in other countries, they do not seek an illusory
emancipation based on demands for rights which can only
divert them from their essential femininity and which draw
them into an absurd struggle against men. Our women
know that they have won dignity and the deep respect of all
Chileans, they know that theirs is the most venerable and
admirable role of all.[2]

During this tribute, the wife of General Pinochet made a
speech in which she referred extensively to the role of
bourgeois women in the counter-revolution against Popular
Unity; naturally she forgot to make any mention of the part
played by working-class and progressive women in building
popular power. As she describes it, 'Women saw the
looming threat of slavery, reacted and took to the streets to
demand liberty for themselves and their sons. This
awareness of the danger of the foreign doctrine provided
our soldiers with the moral backing they needed to take
charge of the destiny of our nation at a time when it was
threatened by the most dreadful tyranny.' What emerges
most clearly here is the social structure envisaged by the
Junta. Each social group is to fulfil a specific function in
the system. Women are to provide the sensitivity and
inspiration which will lead the nation (the men) to take
correct decisions. The nation (the men) will respond to the
call of the traditional values (embodied in the women) and
will rise to defend them. The result should be complete
ideological coherence.

In the 1 December 1973 issue of *Ecrilla* Luiz Hernandez
Parker, a noted political commentator, asserted that 'unlike
men, women do not make political calculations, only
human calculations'. In other words, the mass media tell
women that they must present only demands which are in
keeping with the status they have been granted. On 20 May
1975 the *Mercurio* published a petition addressed to Lucia
Hiriart de Pinochet during the first women's convention
held in Jemuco to celebrate International Women's Year.

The petition called for 'a law which will grant an allowance to housewives who have no other wages'. It also demanded that creches be set up and that work of a kind that women could accomplish at home be provided. Such demands are exactly what one would expect from 'our Chilean women'. They perpetuate a system of dependency which relegates women to a subordinate position; a woman imprisoned and exploited in her own home serves as the perfect symbol for the most reactionary kind of capitalism. From 11 September 1973 onwards, the military Junta set about destroying many social, political and cultural institutions. Thousands of state employees were sacked and replaced by officers whose main task was to maintain a high level of repression and surveillance. Part of the Army was officially detached to take over roles previously carried out by civilians. A women's army corps was then created in order to fill the resulting gaps in the military hierarchy's own bureaucracy. The official function allocated to this new women's corps was 'to give women an opportunity to realize a military vocation and to help in the tasks specific to the Army'. In his speech commemorating the first anniversary of the Javiera Carrera Military Academy, its Director, Colonel Alfredo Rehen, presented his own view of women's contribution to military activities:

> Right from the start of your military education, we, your officers and teachers, will try to show you what is great and noble about the military life. Our heroic sacrifice, our gift to Chile, is based on sublime dedication to the flag, the focus of all our glorious aspirations and all our military vows. We are also fully aware that women must cherish the precious qualities God has endowed them with. Each candidate must therefore be a living picture of femininity, without neglecting due military form, of course.

Traditionally, the military have represented their main qualities as courage, honesty, heroism, courtesy and a few other 'virtues' which fit in with the machist image and the authoritarian relationship between officers and men. It was found possible to produce women in a new subaltern role, that of policewoman and spy. The DINA (the Chilean Gestapo) was quick to recruit women as interrogators and torturers, while the government also instituted a kind of military service for women, on the same lines as in Franco's Spain. The 27 July 1974 editorial in *La Tercera* noted:

> The Government is considering a period of compulsory military service for women. The idea is to orient Chilean women's anxieties, to instill in them basic notions of child care, first aid, dietetics and patriotism; certificates of aptitude to be a wife and mother will be issued to all those women who have shown they are ready to take an active part in the life of the nation. Compulsory military service for women is not a mere governmental caprice, it is an unavoidable national necessity. The responsibility of training future workers and housewives cannot be left to the technical schools and families. Every Chilean woman must have a genuine understanding of life and its problems.

Meanwhile Lucia Hiriart de Pinochet[3] could be heard telling the women of Antofagasta that:

> Destiny and the hand of God has placed me, alongside my husband, before a difficult task. I want to restore to 'Our Woman' the dignity of which a conspiracy of lies and false promises has tried to rob her. Thank heavens that at the crucial moment 'the Chilean woman' raised her voice and demanded to be left in peace, to be allowed to think freely and to take her own decisions as to how she and her children ought to live, at a time when foreign manoeuvres inspired by hatred and infamy were striving to constrain her.

How much more mystifying can one get? Pinochet speaks of freedom of thought in a country where books are burnt and *Don Quixote* is banned. His wife talks of 'hatred' and 'infamy' in referring to the Popular Unity Government, whose failure was arguably the failure to pursue its enemies, which sacked nobody for holding different political opinions, and which shed not one drop of blood.

Bourgeois Chilean women were, in any case, soon put in their place by the new regime. A few were given official posts but in society as a whole it became much more difficult for women to integrate into the male-dominated professional world. As *El Mercurio* put it on 26 June 1972 in

an article entitled 'Women's Mission': 'Women's role is to
control family consumption, just as it is men's role to carry
out the process of production.'

The Junta was soon appealing once more to women who
were bearing the full weight of the economic crisis now
affecting every stratum of society. The same middle-class
women who were suspicious of the measures implemented
by Popular Unity, fearing that they might become
proletarianized, now face a steady decline in their standard
of living. It was this particular stratum Pinochet was
addressing when he said, 'Chilean women are putting up
with all these strains in order to save our balance of trade
and our economy. They deserve everybody's admiration
and congratulations for their efforts. We ask women to be
patient: 1974 is a year of sacrifice; 1975 will be a year of
rest.' Unfortunately, facts are stubborn. The steadily rising
unemployment and increased poverty of 1975 and 1976
imply that many further tests are in store for the patience
of the Chilean people.

As unemployment grows, so the wage discrimination
against women gets worse, at a time when it is more and
more difficult to maintain a home. Faced with this double
reality, many young adolescents are turning to prostitution
and begging.

During Popular Unity, women participated fully in the
activities of the mass movements; they watched over the
distribution of goods through the Price and Supply
Committees and played a militant role within the political
parties. However it must be admitted that Popular Unity
did not manage to develop the specifically female aspects
of the social struggle. The strength of the opposition and
the scale of the problems facing the Government led it to
put off efforts to raise women's consciousness till later.
Women therefore remained fixed in their role as reprod-
ucers of the labour force. The tragic fate of the Chilean
Left has certainly raised women's consciousness of their
own situation and of the concrete problems they face: after
the coup, a great many women had no choice but to take
over the traditionally male task of ensuring their family's
survival. An April 1975 article in the Mexican paper
Excelsior illustrates the role of contemporary Chilean
women in the struggle for liberation:

Chilean women are organizing to struggle, knowing full well
the risks they run even when they try to provide material
assistance to those most in need. They know that the
struggle may land them in jail or in the cemetery. But their
despair is so intense that they cannot just sit back and watch
what is happening. It is still far better to take risks than to
bear the present situation passively. Chilean women have
learnt that they have a social role, and this awareness is
irreversible for it has been acquired through pain and will
never be denied.

Notes

1. The measure was proposed a few days after the coup but
   was soon dropped. Even the women who supported the
   military junta objected.
2. *El Mercurio*, 27 July 1975.
3. Lucia de Pinochet, *La Tercera*, Santiago de Chile, 1 February
   1975.

Colombia: Family Law and Legal Reform

With an area of 1,139,000 square kilometres, about twice the size of France, Colombia lies in the north of South America, bordering on Ecuador, Peru and Brazil to the south and Venezuela to the east. Its 2,600 kilometres of Pacific and Caribbean coastline stretch down either side of the Panama Isthmus. Most of the 24.5 million inhabitants are concentrated in the western part of the country, which is one of the richest and most fertile regions. Three branches of the Andes Cordillera cut across it from north to south. Immense and still largely uncultivated plains stretch eastwards, and the south-east is still almost entirely covered by the Amazonian forest.

Unlike most Latin American countries, where all national activity is monopolized by an overgrown capital city, the Colombian economy has developed simultaneously around several urban centres in different parts of the country. One effect has been the development of marked cultural differences between the regions in behaviour, ways of thinking and attitudes towards women's role and participation in social life.

Along with Venezuela, Colombia is one of the only South American republics to have preserved a 'democratic' system of representative government in the Western sense of the word. But this system has remained very fragile, mainly because of the country's serious economic and social inequalities which have led, throughout Colombia's history, to innumerable popular revolts and riots, savagely repressed on each occasion.

The traditionalist character of the country can be largely attributed to the influence of the Catholic Church not only

in educational and cultural matters but also in social
organization, politics and even economic affairs.

A New Legal Status for Women

In December 1974 the Colombian Government passed 71
articles of a new law on the family, aimed at 'improving the
judicial status of the family and eliminating various odious
and ancestral types of discrimination between the sexes'.[1]
This reform, along with other 'feminist'-oriented measures,
was part of the programme proposed by the new President
in his election manifesto. Yet, despite the increasing
number of women engaged in the legal profession, only
one woman jurist actually took part in drawing up this new
statute which, if one is to believe the present President,
Lopez Michelsen, was supposed to 'eliminate all forms of
discrimination against women'.[2]

In contrast with the old fundamentally machist civil code
which defined women as minors and made them legally
'inferior', the new statute naturally seemed very bold. For
the first time, 'the rights, obligations and legal status of
Colombian women, within the family, the home and society
at large, are defined on a basis of equality with men.'[3] 'The
aim is to ensure that neither of the partners in a marriage
should enjoy special advantages, and that both partners can
play an equal part in managing the affairs of their family.'[4]

To achieve this, certain existing laws were revoked,
notably those constraining women to full obedience to
their husbands. With the repeal of Article 1504, women
ceased to be 'legal incapables'.[5] For the first time extra-
marital sexual activity by either husband or wife became a
valid reason for separation. Until then, male adultery was
institutionalized and accepted, and separation proceedings
could be filed only if a man took to living with his mistress
or if a woman committed adultery.

Progressive as they were, the new measures did not
completely eradicate the old situation. The penal code, for
instance, still stipulates that a man may be acquitted of
murder if he kills his wife when, having caught her
committing adultery, he is 'beside himself with anger and
despair'. No such indulgence is granted to women, who are

cast as mere 'resting places' of the family's honour, morality and dignity, as defined by men in their role as heads of the family hierarchy.

Since 1976 legal divorce has been possible, but the restrictions imposed on the civil law by the Concordat between the Vatican and the Colombian state make it extremely difficult in practice. Under the 1886 Constitution, Catholicism was declared the state religion, making divorce absolutely forbidden even for civil marriages. Providing it had been celebrated 'in accordance with the stipulations of the Council of Trent', a Catholic marriage enjoyed full legal status.[6] It was indissoluble, compulsory for all baptized citizens—in other words for most Colombians—and legally binding on the persons and goods of the couple and their descendants.

In order to bring the new law on divorce into effect, the Concordat of 1887 had to be replaced.[7] A new Concordat between the Church and Colombia was drawn up in 1973 and approved by Congress in 1974. Just as anachronistic and anti-Constitutional as its predecessor, the new version did present certain advantages, in that all Colombians can now opt for civil marriage without having to abjure the Catholic religion.[8] Such a marriage has the same status in law as a Catholic marriage, but Catholic marriage itself remains indissoluble in law.[9] Those who have separated before the new laws still cannot remarry; the only option open to them continues to be civil marriage abroad.

It is important to stress that, although there is a sense in which all Colombian women—be they workers, peasants, secretaries, housewives, academics, lawyers, doctors, engineers or 'society ladies'—suffer from problems common to all women, they are nonetheless not all affected in the same way. Everything depends on their social situation and the economic position they occupy, and this is particularly true in the case of divorce. Even if it does in principle offer a solution to a certain social problem, divorce in practice only concerns a minority of the female population, mainly from the upper and middle classes, since amongst the poor people generally tend to live together unmarried.

There is thus really not much to be expected from a piece of family legislation which itself remains subordinate to a Concordat granting special privileges to the ecclesiastical courts and which in practice only legitimizes the domination and misuse of power by authorities whose existence dates back to the colonial era. For instance, Article 1 of the 1974 Concordat lays down that the state 'considers the Apostolic, Roman and Catholic religion as a fundamental element in the common well-being and in the integral development of the community.'[10] Thanks to this clause, the Church, which has a long history of close association with political power, to say the least, can continue to exercise its powers of coercion: the State guarantees the Church the right to veto government decisions whenever it considers that this 'integral development' is threatened. This amounts to ratifying the Catholic Church's interference in every sphere of national life, be it spiritual, educational or even economic.

Let us take a concrete example of what this can mean. Recently, the Catholic hierarchy of Risaralda vetoed the appointment of Dora Luz de Botero as Governor of the *Département* on the grounds that she had contracted a second civil marriage. The Church construed this as 'social behaviour offensive to a people's dignity'.[11] While not sharing the Church's opinion, President Lopez was forced to concede. 'The [ensuing] scandal has damaged the reputation of a wife and mother; the Government has perhaps injured [this lady] by appointing her, in her capacity as an expert on literacy, to carry out the Government's experimental literacy programme in Risaralda.' Later in the same announcement, he says, 'If, *after having been subjected to such unchristian treatment*, after having been refused nomination merely *because she had been divorced* and had then contracted a civil marriage, rather *than remain single or live with someone unofficially*, [this lady] prefers not to accept the post, *I will gladly replace her with some other citizen, male or female.*'[12]

Applying the new family legislation to the guidance and education of children has also been limited by the demands of the Concordat. But still it did mark the first occasion when both spouses were entrusted with this responsibility, while another reform laid down that all the responsibilities involved in bringing up children, choosing a place to live and organizing the family budget should be shared equally between the parents. (Any serious disputes can be brought before a judge.) Furthermore, 'husbands and wives must do their best to fulfil the necessary domestic tasks' and 'if they keep separate accounts whilst living together, they must each contribute to the upkeep of the family in proportion to their income.'

In practice, of course, men usually get out of doing any of the housework. Even if there were once objective historical reasons for a social division of labour based on sex, these conditions have now changed. Yet society continues to allocate specific tasks to men and women under a system of values which supports male supremacy and the social marginalization of women and in which housework is neither appreciated nor recognized as real work. It is presented as one of the 'duties' which women 'naturally' take on. Despite the legal reforms, many men feel that their dignity and masculinity would suffer if they started helping with such work. Furthermore, the law's insistence that men contribute to the domestic budget is seen as an infringement of a man's traditional role as the 'master' whose only 'duty' is to hand out such 'favours' as paying for the food and clothing of his own children.

The statute does hold that children now owe respect and obedience to both parents, thereby departing from the traditional prerogatives allowed to the father in any dispute. The law also stipulates that 'the parents of children born out of wedlock will enjoy the same rights as the parents of legitimate children if the family lives together. If only one parent lives with the child, that parent will assume the rights in question.' This looks like an advance in ensuring that both parents will assume responsibility for the child. But 'in practice, men often delegate the education and emotional support of the children to the women, keeping themselves at a distance even though they take care of the family's economic needs.'[13] This is particularly true when a married woman stays at home to concentrate on family affairs, as if she could counterbalance her economic weakness and her dependence on her husband by devotion to domestic 'duty'. In such cases, there can be no social equality, especially if the woman does not have any of the right qualifications to get a job outside the home. Although the law deals with the question of illegitimate children, the situation of unmarried women who live with a man is far worse than that of married women. Yet this has not been covered at all by the new legislation, even though a very large percentage of Colombian families live in this type of *'de facto* patrimonial society'.[14]

There are already several labour laws and family code recommendations promoting women's incorporation into production, but in fact these measures are rarely applied. To begin with, there has been a steady devalorization of the traditional female occupations: the increase in the number of women in certain sectors of the economy is directly proportional to the vacancies created by men leaving because the jobs are too poorly paid. Women's wages are lower and generally speaking women are offered less responsible jobs. Despite the legal independence of married women, they are rarely economically independent of their husbands; usually they depend on their husbands' wages and are rarely sufficiently educated to be able to break away from the 'guardianship' of the family. Obviously this limits their capacity to assume social responsibility.

Social security benefits are restricted to certain specific categories of workers. Women's low level of involvement in productive (non-domestic) work thus has indirect and long-term repercussions on their health. Where a husband does not have adequate means at his disposal when his wife falls ill, she is barely protected; the best she can expect is the inadequate care provided by the public hospitals, whose services are worse than mediocre due to 'lack of funds'. Present health policy is entirely geared to workers in firms affiliated to social security schemes. Colombia provides no social security system for part-time workers, even though many women who are forced to bring their children up alone have no choice but to take on this type of work. In 1971, there were 550,000 domestic servants in Colombia, most of them women. This group too is not entitled to social security, although they can register for voluntary insurance schemes. As for housewives, they are not protected either, since Article 6 of Law 90 (1946) makes it impossible for women at home to insure themselves directly. They have no right to any state assistance except maternity benefits. (These benefits also apply to unmarried women, but only if the man involved is himself insured.)[15]

Women and the Dominant Ideology

As we have seen, the new family code fails to deal with many problems arising from the social situations women find themselves in. The code applies mainly to married women, especially to housewives whose principal role is to reproduce minutely the very social values which keep them locked into the traditional position of 'inferiority'. Even advances in women's education are potentially affected by this dynamic. All too often women who can afford to go to university are less concerned with acquiring a specific training or body of knowledge than with passing the time until they can get married, since marriage is their only real guarantee of social status and recognition. Considering as well the generally low level of women's education in Colombia, it becomes apparent that even those women who have secured high office are still the victims of unjust socio-economic conditions. Even so, most women who gain access to these privileges come from the wealthiest classes or are directly related to the ruling class.

We have not even mentioned the level of exploitation which the bourgeoisie (both men and women) impose on working women who are often the sole providers for their families. Nor have we dealt with the machist values which have particularly deep roots in a patriarchal and conservative society such as Colombia.[16] These characteristics are accentuated by the implicit misogyny of the Christian sexual ethic and by the decisive influence Catholicism has had on the country's social, cultural and political history.

One might also analyse the concept of 'honour' embodied in certain sections of the penal code. In certain circumstances, where it is a case of 'preserving' someone's 'honour', the anti-abortion provisions may be suspended; the class bias and hypocrisy involved in those exceptions are clear. Meanwhile, hundreds of poor and uneducated women die every year as a result of backstreet abortions. Apparently they have no 'honour' to lose, so the law makes no provision for them.

Abortion, along with prostitution, is a serious social

problem. In Colombia, between 76,000 and 150,000
abortions are carried out every year. In 1970, there were
128,700 abortions. According to the statistics gathered at
the San Juan de Dios Hospital and the Bogota Materno-
Infantil Institute,[17] most requests for abortion come from
married women (two-thirds of all patients) in economic
difficulty. Sixty-six per cent of induced abortions leading to
hospitalization were carried out by abortionists with no
medical training. The precarious economic status of many
women, ignorance of birth control methods and moral
strictures condemning control of fertility have led to a
situation in which there are two clandestine abortions for
every four children born. The unhygienic conditions in
which these backstreet abortions take place kill more
women than do complications in delivery. In 1971 two
women died every week in the hospitals of Bogota
following botched abortions.[18]

The phenomenon of prostitution, including child
prostitution, reflects economic imbalances and types of
social disintegration in the country, but it also stands as an
indictment of the negative role played by the Church's
conceptions of 'virginity' and 'maternity'. Social taboos
involving women's 'purity' and 'decency' reinforce these
conceptions. For many adolescent girls who have 'broken
the rules' by losing their virginity, and who have in
consequence been thrown out by their families, prostitution
is the only option. In other cases the roots of prostitution
can be traced back to destitution, overcrowded housing,
desertion and the white slave trade.

The Family Code and Social Realities

Although the new laws are a definite step forwards, their
intention is frequently frustrated by social realities. In
order to understand the limits of the statute, one must take
into account the enormous gap between the legal and the
political institutions of the country, as well as various
economic and social realities. In other words, one must be
aware of the distinction between 'a democratic state' and 'a
democratic society'.[19] Women's suffrage is a good example:

> In Colombia, women did not win universal suffrage through
> their own struggles: it was granted because of the political
> situation at the time. Women were used to bring about a
> period of peace following an era of political violence.
> Women's conservatism was a guarantee of stability for the
> system. The country had recently emerged from dictatorship.
> In 1957, the new regime had to be legitimized. Increasing
> the number of electors increased the number of votes.[20]

Nonetheless, the high percentage of absentions has still
not significantly diminished.

Clearly, the conception of women's problems embodied
in the family code neglects a great many important themes,
including the sexual division of labour, discrimination in
education, the need for creches and social services to
facilitate women's access to professional independence,
unequal wages, the position of women in production and in
the trade union movement, etc. The problems of peasant
women are also inadequately analysed, despite the fact that,
because of Colombia's particular agricultural structure,
they have become an indispensable element in the
economic process. Indeed, according to the latest census,
Colombian peasant women are 25 per cent of the total
population.[21]

A report on the views of 140 women from the
countryside gives some idea of the needs and frustrations of
the peasantry.[22] They feel 'marginalized because they are
women and because of the social structures; marginalized
because they are peasant women, who more than any
others of their sex are excluded from the life of the
community, even though their presence is necessary in
agriculture production; marginalized because they are
amongst the poorest people in the country.'[23] In the urban
areas, working-class women face similar problems compounded by the effects of the rural exodus of women from
the countryside who pour into the towns, find it impossible
to get a job and swell the ranks of the unemployed.

In conclusion, the law will only achieve its objectives if it
can find a practical way to help that majority of women
who are still largely illiterate and 'enslaved not only by the
system of capitalist exploitation but also by traditions
which keep them on the margins of the economy and social

life and relegate them to housework, sexual servitude and biological reproduction'.²⁴ At the moment, the majority of Colombian women still bear the full brunt of a repressive cultural tradition and the even greater burden of economic exploitation.

Witness by a Popular Leader

Carmen de Rodriguez, a popular leader from the eastern districts of Bogota, has dedicated herself to the struggle for working-class rights during the last thirty years. What follows is an extract from an interview she granted to Alternativa *magazine on 16 September 1974 (No. 16).*

Alternativa: What is the main problem facing Colombian women?
Carmen de Rodriguez: Education puts many restraints on women. Children are told that the Army is there to defend the nation, for instance. We are the victims of an education geared to make us submit. Women have never received the kind of education which would enable them to understand their class situation, and that there are really only two classes, the exploiters and the exploited. Furthermore, the gross ideological content of radio broadcasts, films and television programmes keeps women stupefied and prevents them from realizing the importance of studying history.
Alternativa: What do you think of the Government's plans to control the cost of living?
Carmen de Rodriguez: The capitalist class is insatiable. In the factories, the bosses are constantly seeking to increase their profits. How? By putting up prices; but then the people can no longer buy anything. They know that the population is growing. Machines are replacing people. We are already no longer worth anything to them. Their response is to try to eliminate us altogether, through hunger. They put up the cost of living and try to control the birth rate—not because they feel sorry for the poor, of course. If that were so, they wouldn't exploit us so much. If I were paid decent wages for the work I do, I could have as many children as I want, and they would be well fed and well educated. But the capitalist class knows that the poor amongst the population are increasing daily. They are well aware that the more discontented poor people there are,

the more dangerous it is for them. The bosses can see the 'monster' growing; what they want is to be a majority in order to dominate the people. Alberto Lleras, who has disseminated these theories, has earned his nickname: people call him Mr. Pill. All this comes from over there [the U.S.], they propose the solutions and the people over here accept them. People with money are the same everywhere. There is supposedly not enough food available to feed everybody, yet this country is full of unexploited land and unemployed people. In China, they have a population of about 900 million, all of whom are adequately nourished and educated. People who have liberated themselves are like that. But here, where there is so much wealth, people are dying in the streets.

Every night, at the gates of the Archbishop's palace, you can see three or four old people who have dossed down there. But it doesn't disturb the Archbishop. Everything the Church tells you is nothing but lies. Have you ever seen a poor Archbishop? Just look at how they live, with their cars, their robes . . . The Church has always been on the side of the exploiters. It is an obscurantist institution which tells the poor to be patient and to submit, because they will inherit the Kingdom of God hereafter. But what we want is to live decently now, not to starve and want all the time. Nobody has ever come down from heaven to tell me how things are up there. But in this world, God's ministers rob and exploit the people. They have far more than any sinner. And they use people's religious feeling to enrich themselves.

Religion has also been one of the most powerful methods used to impose inferiority on women. The marriage ceremony tells us to 'be subject to man'. We are treated just like things. Women are kept as long as they are useful, and then thrown away. Our value has never been recognized. As women, we ought to bring children into the world and bring them up to serve their class. Women must give their offspring a political education which will prepare them to struggle for another system. We must bring children into the world to fight, not to be enslaved and humiliated.

Liberation consists of understanding and recognizing one's own worth, in understanding that this worth can be used to serve the class struggle. Liberation is not a struggle against men, but a fight to be able to struggle side by side with them, at work and in the battle to build socialism together.

Notes

1. 'El nuevo estatuto de la familia', Decreto 2820/74, *El Tiempo*, Bogota, 22 December 1974, p. 23.
2. *Ibid.*
3. *Ibid.*
4. *Ibid.*, p. 24.
5. 'Legal incapables' include all those who live under the legal guardianship of somebody else (children, the mentally ill and women).
6. Article 17 of the 1887 Concordat. The Council of Trent (1545) elevated marriage to the status of a sacrament, an indissoluble bond and contract and a 'divine institution'. Even the law had to remain bound by the will of the Church and divorce became impossible.
7. This Concordat was accepted by Law 35 of 1888.
8. Until the promulgation of Law 54 in 1924, the so-called Concha Law named after the Colombian President who sponsored it, civil marriage automatically entailed the excommunication not only of the couple, but also of the judges, witnesses and secretaries involved since, in keeping with Article 17, they were all deemed to have violated the Concordat. Law 54 laid down that the first part of Article 17 should not be applied if the couple concerned declared before their marriage that they had formally broken with the Church and the Catholic religion. The procedure established to this end flagrantly contradicted Article 53 of the Constitution, which states that 'the State guarantees all citizens freedom of conscience, belief and worship within the bounds of Christian morality and the law of the land.' It is worth stressing that the Constitution does not mention Catholic *dogma* or *religion*, only 'Christian morality'. There is clearly an acute contradiction between the Concordat and the Charter of the Constitution. Furthermore, the process of abjuration itself involved submitting to an extensive interrogation, which was quite out of keeping with the other liberties guaranteed by the Constitution. The abjuration required by law was public and solemn, and a declaration of the couple's formal break with the Church had to be submitted in writing to a magistrate. This declaration was then incorporated into the marriage bans, posted in the town hall and the parish, and sent to the local church representative. Finally, the declaration had to be ratified by the couple during the marriage itself, which could only be held one month after it had been presented. See 'El Concordato', *La Nueva Economía*, Bogota, 1973.

9. Andres Holguin,'Matrimonio y divorcio en unEstado confesional', *El Tiempo*, 'Lectura dominical', Bogota, 6 April 1975.
10. *Ibid*.
11. 'Message from President M. Lopez to the bishops of Pereira (Risaralda) on the occasion of the vetoing of the new governor', *El Espectador*, Bogota, 5 March 1975.
12. *Ibid*., p. 3–A, our italics.
13. 'Declaraciones del Ministro de Justicia sobre los nuevas reformas constitucionales', *El Tiempo*, Bogota, 23 December 1974.
14. Virginia Gutierrez de Pineda, *La familia en Colombia*, Bogota: Universidad Nacional, 1965. (There are no more recent studies on the subject.) The high number of illegitimate children can be deduced from the following figures: according to Virginia Gutierrez de Pineda, an anthropologist, unmarried couples in 1964 variously represented from 0 to 20 per cent of all unions in the central and eastern regions of the country. On the Caribbean and Pacific Coast, the percentages were 60 and 80 per cent respectively, while in certain areas inland from the Atlantic Coast and in the south (Pays, Valle, Cauca and Narino) the figure was a little over 40 per cent.
15. Alfred Mallet, *Les femmes et la sécurité sociale en Amerique Latine*, Geneva: I.L.O., 1975.
16. The Colombian Civil Code, derived directly from Roman Law, puts women in a position which confirms the role of the patriarchal structure in maintaining the legally and institutionally absolute authority of the father or husband over his wife and children (extension of the old property law). It was only under the new Family Code of 1974 that women ceased to be legal 'incapables'. But despite the reforms, the machist mentality and the dominant classes' system of values still persists.
17. Santamaria Luis Eduardo, 'Estudio sobre el aborto', *Revista Colombiana de Obstetricia y Ginecología*, March 1970.
18. Parra Nohra, 'Seminario de Población,' *El Espectador*, Bogota, 3 June 1973.
19. Quoted in Jorge E. Ruiz, 'Situación del escritor en Colombia', *Mito 1955–1962*, Bogota: Bibl. colombiana de cultura, 1975, p. 66.
20. Pinzón Gomez Patricia, *Comportamiento politico femenino* (unpublished thesis), Bogota: Dept. of Political Science, Universidad de los Andes, 1972, p. 29, our italics.
21. In Colombia in 1972 the *per capita* income was U.S. $328. The distribution by sector of the economically active population in 1967 was as follows: agriculture 47.3 per cent; industry 18.3 per cent; services 30.6 per cent. In 1972, 26.6 per cent of the G.N.P. was produced by the agricultural sector.
22. Investigation conducted by the 10th Congress Commission

as a contribution to International Women's Year and
published by the President's Office.

23. Patricia Lozano, 'La mujer de la otra Colombia', *El Espectador*,
Bogota, 31 August 1975.
24. Araújo, Helena, 'Carta sobre el problema de la explosion
demográfica y el control de natalidad', *Alternativa*, No. 18,
Bogota, 1974.

Cuba: Women and the Process of Liberation

> *We live in a socialist country,*
> *we made our revolution sixteen*
> *years ago, but can we really say*
> *that Cuban women have in*
> *practice gained equal rights with*
> *men and that they are fully*
> *integrated into Cuban society?*[1]

This passage expresses a worry which re-emerges time and again, both in the speeches of the Prime Minister Fidel Castro and in the debates of the trade unions and other mass organizations.

Part of the effort to genuinely incorporate Cuban women into social production centres around attempts to overcome certain objective material obstacles to that integration. The state has set up creches, nursery schools, automatic laundries, workers' canteens, a system of grants and semi-boarding schools; medical services are available in every part of the country and the government has approved health and safety at work regulations. These and many other measures have done a great deal to lighten the burden that women once had to bear alone. Also, the lifting of a series of legal restrictions limiting male and female employment opportunities has contributed to revalorizing the role of women in society.[2] Encouraging women to take a more active role has taken the concrete form of measures to facilitate their effective incorporation into production. Further efforts are under way to resolve the remaining material difficulties and to raise the level of women's technical and academic training, so that their growing demand to be fully incorporated into production can be satisfied.

Even so, these initiatives have not achieved a complete transformation of society's traditional conception of women. A mentality littered with prejudices and old cultural habits inherited from the past still persists to prevent women from developing their capacities to the full and participating in social life as equals who enjoy the same rights and responsibilities as men.

Women and Political Leadership

The problem became particularly clear during the elections to the Popular Power Assembly in Matanzas Province. Only 7.6 per cent of the candidates proposed by the masses, and only 3 per cent of those actually elected, were women. Both the Revolutionary Government and the Federation of Cuban Women (F.C.W.) wanted to know why the number of women proposed and elected was so small, even though half the population are women. The F.C.W. conducted an investigation which produced some very illuminating results.[3]

The investigation revealed that most full-time political representatives were men and that women's political work, however important, was rarely their main activity. When men who had occupied positions of political leadership were asked why they had dropped them, the most frequent answer was because they had been offered work elsewhere or because they had retired. But for women the reason was often that domestic duties and care of their children did not leave them enough time to assume other responsibilities. Illness, either their own or of a member of the family, was also often mentioned.

The electors were then asked what they saw as the factors which prevented women from occupying leadership posts. The most frequent replies were as follows: Firstly, that women had a responsibility to look after their children, their husband and their home. Secondly, that they lacked the cultural and political training to take on the task of leadership. Thirdly, that their health was more delicate, or that it was part of their job to look after anybody in the family who fell ill. Fourthly, that their husbands, fiances or fathers did not approve or allow them to play a political role. Fifthly, that men did not understand that it was important for women to participate in social life. Sixthly, that women did not like to lead, and indeed underestimated their own capacities and the role they could play in society. Finally, that people simply preferred to see men occupy leadership positions.

The same answers cropped up repeatedly throughout the course of the investigation. For example, people were asked why should a woman not be proposed as leader of the Popular Assembly. The main reasons given were domestic duties, responsibility for children, women's low cultural level and their fear of assuming unfamiliar responsibilities. Some people also answered that men were more capable leaders than women. Old conceptions re-surfaced: husbands, fiances and fathers would disapprove or forbid women to carry out such tasks; women did not really like to lead, etc. For a woman to be a good leader the requirements were set particularly high. 45.6 per cent of respondents said that a woman would have to be 'serious, decent and highly moral', and that she would also have to manage to fulfil her domestic and family responsibilities. This last condition did not apply to men, according to most respondents.

Asked why more women were not proposed as candidates for the Popular Assembly, many people answered that women did not have enough time to spare because they were too busy looking after their homes and children. Particularly perceptive was the answer that not enough had been done to publicise the possibility of choosing women and promoting an awareness of their abilities. These two answers were often given when people were asked why the women who had been proposed were not chosen. Other replies invoked discrimination against women and men's refusal to be governed by women.

The investigation revealed that 45.7 per cent of women interviewed were in fact willing to assume leadership positions. The remaining 54.3 per cent gave lack of qualifications and inadequate schooling as their main reason for reluctance. Backward conceptions such as 'women do not like to lead' or 'that sort of responsibility should be exercised by men' did not often turn up, but people frequently referred to the fact that it was more 'difficult' for women to assume a leadership role. These answers reveal the effects of the old education system, which taught women to consider themselves incapable of assuming important responsibilities outside the house. The fact that women are still expected to do all the housework and bring up the children severely restricts their exercise of other socially useful functions. It is at this cultural level that Cuban women are not yet completely liberated. A great deal of ideological work will have to be done before the problem is eliminated, as the Revolutionary Government is well aware. Fidel Castro admitted it openly during the Second Congress of the F.C.W. in November 1974:

> And what do these figures show? That after fifteen years of revolution we are still politically and culturally backward in this field. It is patently obvious that there are still objective and subjective factors which maintain the discrimination against women.[4]
>
> But we must bear in mind the subjective factors, the problems inherited from an old culture, the old habits and old prejudices.[5]
>
> It is becoming clearer and clearer that women must participate in the struggle against exploitation, imperialism, colonialism, neo-colonialism and racism, in short that they must participate in the struggle for national liberation. But when the objective of national liberation has been attained, women must continue to struggle for their own liberation within human society.[6]

Some changes are already under way and this can be seen in the fact that the investigation brought out certain significant contradictions in the responses; a new way of looking at things is establishing itself conceptually but has not yet filtered through in practice. For instance, 58.9 per cent agreed that a woman should take on a leadership role even if her husband or father objected. When asked who should be responsible for bringing up children, 1.7 per cent of interviewees answered men, 28 per cent said women and 70.3 per cent thought the responsibility should be shared. In answer to a question as to who in a family should take the important decisions, 3.9 per cent thought it should be the woman, 38.3 per cent said the man and 57.8 per cent recognized that joint decisions were preferable. 63.9 per cent of interviewees thought that if women could not undertake leadership tasks as easily as men, it was because of their domestic workload.

Machist and discriminatory conceptions did emerge, however, the moment men were asked why they did not do their share of housework. They felt that housework was a woman's job and feared the strictures and mockery of their fellows. Some men felt that this sort of work was too simple for them and that their neighbours would think they were dominated by their wife. Asked if women should stay at home to look after the children and do the housework, leaving political activity to the men, 51.9 per cent of the interviewees answered Yes and 48.1 per cent No. But 56.4 per cent thought that a married woman ought to carry on studying and/or working. The response is clearly self-contradictory, since a woman burdened with all the family's domestic problems is unlikely to be able to find the time to continue educating herself.

There are in fact already signs of change within the structure of the bourgeois nuclear family. Women's participation in productive labour, their more or less extended absence from the home for periods of voluntary work, and their active role in the street level Revolutionary Defence Committees have modified the traditional couple relationships which are now founded more on mutual respect and less on tradition.

The Family Code and Social Change

The 1974 Family Code played a considerable role in this development by establishing equality between men and women as the rule in marriage. Marriage itself lost its institutional character and became simply a permanent and voluntary union between a man and a woman. Both husband and wife have the same rights over the family's assets. The Family Code specifically guarantees the participation of both men and women in the economic, cultural and political order of the country. Within the nuclear family, men and women have a duty to help each other. Men are enjoined to contribute to their wife's personal and intellectual development and to share in all the housework. Both partners have the same obligations and duties concerning the protection, upbringing, support and education of their children.

The Family Code is not a simple piece of formal legislation. On the contrary, it was widely debated amongst the rank and file, in the Revolutionary Defence Committee, at work, and elsewhere before it was passed. The debates around the Code gave women an opportunity to discuss the issues, first amongst themselves, and at work, and then in mixed groups. Women seized the opportunity to express many long-standing grievances. Digna Cire, the leader of the Women's Front of Cuban Workers Congress,[7] declared that there were still far too many revolutionaries who thought that a woman's place was in the home and that men belonged in the outside world. She added that in many cases men were the last remaining obstacle to women's liberation. For Cuban women, the way to resolve these problems was through joint action with men, with the working masses. She pointed out that assemblies had been organizing to this end, since individual discussions with fathers or husbands were no longer enough.

In the workplace debates which ensued, women complained about their male comrades' lack of co-operation in domestic and family matters. Women pointed out that they were being asked to join the vanguard of the working class, without any recognition of the fact that they had to cope with all the housework. Efforts are now being made to work through this new stage in the ideological struggle within Cuban society.

It is worth stressing that it is only since the Revolution that the problems of discrimination against women have been brought into the open and made an issue of public concern. This was the real beginning of awareness of the issues and their efforts to cope with them. This process of liberation was one of the 1959 Revolution's most important contributions.

Children of both sexes now receive the same kind of education from the moment they enter a creche. At first, Cuba was desperately short of qualified staff for both creches and nursery schools. Today, there is a staff training college providing a four-year course in psychology, physical education, dietetics, pedagogy, etc. One aspect of the curriculum which has been particularly important in overcoming traditional sex roles is the work-study programme which is now compulsory for all children at every level. This is not to say that some parents do not still pass on a discriminatory education to their children. Traditional images of femininity are still evident in the clothes and toys provided by parents and in the different games they encourage their children to play. But all this is being broken down by the new generation, even if not quite as fast or intensely as one might wish.

For some women over thirty, the fact that they do voluntary work as well as taking responsibility for their home and children on top of their paid job makes them, in their own eyes, the most active militants around. But this is less and less the case for young people who have grown up during the process of the Revolution. Most young women have now rejected the bourgeois idea of marriage and motherhood as the only road to personal fulfilment.

Recently, a campaign against *machismo* was launched in the newspapers, on television and radio, and by posters and films. The message was even picked up in jokes and popular slang. Cubans are facing up to their material and cultural problems, to the fixity and persistence of old ideas. The economic problems of a country trying to liberate itself from underdevelopment and dependence are compounded by the difficulties involved in changing people's attitudes, especially the traditional notions of women's social role, the family and the proper way to bring up children.

The victory of the Revolution has certainly paved the way for complete women's liberation. But until there are certain ideological and cultural changes, the Revolution will be deprived of the full revolutionary potential women can contribute.

Notes

1. Fidel Castro, Closing speech to the 2nd Congress of the Federation of Cuban Women (F.M.C.), 29 November 1974, p. 10.
2. Resolutions 47 and 48, which were originally designed as protective legislation, set aside 500 jobs exclusively for women and 500 for men. These resolutions also took into

account the difficulties experienced by women in meeting
certain productivity norms, and protected women from
certain types of work which might have an adverse effect on
their health, especially when pregnant. Resolutions 47 and 48
were approved in 1968, at a time when Cuba was facing
serious difficulties. The country needed to concentrate its
male labour force in specific sectors of the economy
(construction, hydraulic engineering, etc.) to get it moving
again. The Ministry of Labour, having investigated the
number of jobs occupied by men which could be immediately
filled by women, called on the men to take up new jobs
requiring greater physical effort. However, these resolutions
had the secondary effect of reinforcing the separation
between men and women's activities, thereby perpetuating a
sexually discriminatory division of labour. In 1973, the
situation having changed, the C.T.C., supported by the
F.M.C., called for the revision of the two resolutions and they
were eventually eliminated. In any case, the resolutions were
frequently ignored in practice, as women often executed
many of the tasks 'reserved for men' in the course of
voluntary work.

3. Following the elections for Popular Power in Matanzas
   Province, the F.M.C. decided to conduct an inquiry to find
   out why the masses had proposed so few women as delegates.
   The results were published in 1975 by the Department of
   Revolutionary Orientation of the Central Committee of the
   Communist Party of Cuba, and were presented as an
   appendix to Thesis No. 3 on the exercise of full equality by
   women at the 1st Congress of the P.C.C. (December 1975).
   The report was based on 635 interviews, 302 of which were
   with men. The sample was drawn from the Matanzas electoral
   register and was made up of about 40 men and 40 women
   from each of 10 selected municipalities. The interviews were
   conducted both in the towns (46.5 per cent) and in the
   countryside (34.5 per cent); 66 per cent of interviewees were
   aged less than 45 years, and 34.7 per cent were in the 15 to 30
   age group.

4. Castro, *op. cit.*, p. 12.
5. *Ibid.*, p. 37.
6. *Ibid.*, p. 38.
7. In 1967, the F.M.C. proposed that the existing workplace
   women's delegations be replaced by a Secretariat of the
   Women's Front within the C.T.C., so as to eliminate the
   disjunction between the specific problems of working women
   and the working-class context.

Ecuador: Peasant Women—Exploitation and Resistance

Peasant Women and Productive Labour

The Sierra

Until the Spanish conquered South America, what is today Ecuador was part of the Inca Empire. The social base of the society was the *ayllu*, a group of families linked through marriage or kinship. The family was itself the main economic unit. Each household, consisting of the parents and their unmarried children, formed a unit of production and consumption within which there was a certain division of labour. Women took care of all the housework as well as participating in agricultural labour.

While the Spanish preserved the family and the *ayllu* as the fundamental social structures of post-conquest Ecuador, they made them into the basis of a system of exploitation. The family was taken as the basic unit in the system of taxation or tribute and the head of each family was responsible for paying a regular sum to the Crown. The *caciques*, the headmen of each *ayllu*, were given the responsibility of tax collection, and had to make up any shortfall in the contribution of any individual family within their community.

With this system of tribute the Spanish had found a legal rationale for their extortion of surplus labour and goods from the indigenous population. During the 16th and 17th Centuries, forced labour (*mita*) was used extensively in the mines, in the textile plants (*batanes*) and in the fields and houses owned by the big landlords. Men were brought to work in the mines for periods of six months or more, many never to return, while the women remained behind on the

ayllu's lands, taking sole charge of the fields. It was also
mainly the men who were forced to work in the textile
plants. Again, women had to take over the work in the fields
as well as supplying their husbands with the means to
survive. The community thus provided the goods necessary
for the day-to-day reproduction of the men's labour power,
without which the system of exploitation could not have
carried on functioning.

Entire communities were transplanted in order to
cultivate the Spaniards' lands, and act as personal servants in
the landowners' houses. For the women, these 'services'
often included submission to sexual abuse by the landowner
and his sons; the 'sexual initiation' (*pernada*) of young girls
on the eve of their wedding was the prerogative of the
landed aristocracy. In these ways the indigenous population,
tied as they were to the land, effectively became the
property of the big landowners. The grants of land issued by
the Crown (*encomiendos*) actually included the indigenous
population required to farm it. And because the indigenous
population's obligations to the landlords were so extensive
that the men by themselves could not have met them all,
women came to do a great deal of the work required.

The Huasipungo

During the 17th and 18th Centuries the family continued to
be the basic unit of production, providing the social basis
for the *huasipungo*, (a term derived from the Quechua words
for 'house' and 'door'). The *huasipungo* was the subsistence
land granted by the landlord to an indigenous family in
exchange for the work of household heads in the
landowner's fields. Although they were also supposed to be
paid a salary, in practice they received nothing—each time
the landowner drew up his accounts, the families sank
deeper and deeper into debt. This increasing indebtedness
meant that the workers had to remain on the landowner's
property or face being thrown into a debtors' prison. The
huasipunguera families were completely self-sufficient. They
grew maize, beans, potatoes, and quinoa, looked after
livestock and made their own clothes and tools. On top of
this the family as a whole also had to work in the
landowner's house and participate in *mingas*, communal
labour such as road-building. The technology available to

the *huasipunguera* families was of a very low level and their land usually of poor quality. To survive, the whole family had to work.

The Minifundia

The *huasipungo* and other such precarious forms of land tenure were abolished by the 1964 Agrarian Reform Laws by which the indigenous people became poor peasants, each owning a little plot of land. Although they no longer had to supply the landlord with labour and services, they also lost all right of access to the landlord's grazing grounds, woods and water.

Family work is still the basis of the poorer peasantry's subsistence.[1] Women continue to look after the animals and marketing of products from the family's small plot. They also participate in *mingas*, and in agricultural and artisanal work on top of all their domestic chores.

Women take an active part in agricultural work, especially weeding, sowing and harvesting. The work is usually shared between all the members of an extended family, and other members of the community will help with work that needs to be done on each other's plots. All physically fit women do their share of the work alongside the men. Women's participation in *mingas* includes road-building and repairing, shifting and loading bricks when a school or community centre is built, etc. And on top of all this, it is the women who prepare the meals for the community's workers, toting the ingredients in sacks on their backs, cooking them and serving them.

While the actual productive work done by a peasant woman is recognized as such, her role as 'a woman', as the reproducer of the labour force, is not. Yet in practice the impoverished peasant women of the Sierra have to cope with a double work-load, productive work as well as housework. Even so their importance in production, currently as well as in the past, means that they are not as devalued, oppressed and dominated as ordinary housewives.

For instance, peasant women are almost entirely responsible for marketing their family's produce, a crucial function. 'Women play the key role in selling the produce of the indigenous families. Even if they themselves do not actually sell the goods, their agreement to the price set by their husbands is a decisive factor.' There are usually more women than men buying and selling produce in the local markets.[2]

The Coast

Capitalist agriculture is much more developed in the coastal regions than in the Sierra, based mainly on a system of cash crop plantations (cocoa, coffee, rice, bananas), as opposed to the subsistence farming which prevails in the Sierra. The plantations employ both temporary and permanent wage labourers, although pre-capitalist survivals also exist, for instance the *sembradores*, peasants who clear land not currently in use by the plantations, and then sow it with cocoa, coffee, etc., using plants provided by the plantation. They have the use of the land for a given period (about five years) after which it reverts to the plantation.

The family remains the basic unit of production for both the *sembradores* and the smaller landowners. Women make an essential contribution to the agricultural work involved.

Migration

As time goes by, the small plots of land held by the peasants get even smaller. The holdings are split between the children of a family, while debts sometimes force people to sell off some of their land. These plots eventually become so small that they are incapable of supporting a family, which is then forced to sell part of its labour power in order to survive. The men can sometimes sell their labour to one of the big estates; the women can also hire themselves out as day labourers but usually at half the rate. In any case, the haciendas cannot absorb all the available workers, many of whom therefore have to migrate.

Generally speaking, there are two types of migration: temporary and permanent. Temporary migration involves mainly men, who go to find seasonal work in the coastal plantations or in the mines and the construction industry. These emigrant peasants retain their links with the land and obtain part of their means of subsistence from it. During their absence, their women and children do all the agricultural work. The labour power of these male peasants is thus sold particularly cheap, because part of their means of subsistence still comes from their little plots of land—the work of the families which makes this possible is not taken into account when it comes to determining the men's salaries.

Permanent migration is mainly to the towns, especially Quito and Guayaquil, and usually occurs when an entire family is forced to abandon the land because it can no longer feed itself by subsistence farming. The peasants come to the towns hoping for factory work, which is usually better paid. But the urban industries cannot absorb enough workers, so the migrants are often forced into under-employment (part-time work, work in the retail trade, as porters, etc.) or into unemployment.

In fact women can often find work more easily than men. They usually join the tertiary sector, which is particularly large in Ecuador as in Latin America generally, due to the specific characteristics of these dominated economies. Women can find work as servants, washerwomen, in the retail trade, etc. Amongst the exploited classes in the towns, the woman is often the only salaried member of the family.

It is also fairly common for young girls to migrate to the towns by themselves and find work as servants, thereby lightening the demands on the income from the family plot. Sometimes the girls even contribute part of their scanty wages towards the upkeep of the rest of the family back home.

The family is, as we have seen, the main productive unit amongst the peasantry. This unit survives as such, even during the absence of the men, thanks to the work of the women and children. The family thus does not have the same function as in the developed countries, where it has been stripped of its economic and productive functions and serves only to help reproduce labour power, transmit the dominant ideology and promote consumption.

Of course peasant women are also bound up in the reproduction of labour power and ideology. But the ideology transmitted need not always be the dominant one, and it is important to remember that the peasant family has preserved certain specific ideological characteristics as well as its economic functions. Women are important in these families: they are oppressed, but their oppression is very closely linked to their exploitation and super-exploitation, to the super-exploitation of their families and of the peasantry as a social class. It is only since the peasant family has got caught up in the dominant Western ideology that the oppression of peasant women *as women* has intensified. The children too participate fully in the work and social life of the family. They are not strange, isolated creatures who have nothing to do with adults. On the contrary, they, and their mothers, are respected as individuals, as people each of whom has his or her own economic importance for the family.

Nor is the peasant family an isolated unit in society. It is linked by bonds of friendship (the *compadrazgo*, for instance) and kinship to all the other members of the community, and even to other communities. These links are the practical expression of a peasant solidarity which has existed for centuries and which has not diminished over the years, a solidarity which in fact is growing and gradually becoming a class solidarity.

The Birth Control Programme

Against this background of strong peasant loyalties and respect for women, it becomes all too easy to understand the efforts of certain organizations to enforce 'birth control' programmes based on massive compulsory sterilization of poor women and castration of indigenous children. These foreign organizations—the Peace Corps, the *Amigos de los Americas*, certain Protestant sects, the Mormons, and various foreign advisers to the Ministries of Health, Education and Defence—seek to control the 'growth of the population' in the poorer strata of the nation, in the countryside and in the shanty towns. They claim that 'there are too many people for such a small country'.

Ecuador has a surface area of 280,000 square kilometres and a population of 6,500,000 people (according to the 1974 census)—in other words 12.5 per cent of France's population in an area half the size. Ecuador is also rich in natural resources; it has oil, hundreds of different kinds of fish, gold, wood and fertile land, of which only 46 per cent in the sierra and 63.5 per cent on the coast was being cultivated in 1968 (according to the most recent agricultural census).[3]

109

Although it is quite true that the annual rate of population growth is a high 3.4 per cent,[4] the fundamental problem lies elsewhere: in 1968, 0.78 per cent of the total number of farms accounted for 36 per cent of the arable land, while 75 per cent of all farms occupied only 11 per cent of these lands.[5] Clearly both the misery of the poorer peasantry and the growth of the shanty towns resulting from the rural exodus are consequences of this land monopoly. Reducing the size of the impoverished population through birth control is simply an attempt to relieve social conflicts without dealing with their real cause, neo-colonial exploitation. Yet the bodies involved in this campaign would have us believe that it is population growth which causes poverty.

We must emphasize that we do not question the importance of birth control as such. We are merely trying to show the way it is applied in practice in contemporary Ecuador. Science and technology, like all other forms of knowledge, are used by the country's dominant classes to maintain and reinforce their domination. Birth control is simply a case in point. Imperialism is using these programmes in an attempt to relieve social conflicts and control the supply of manpower, by limiting one of the factors driving the peasants from the countryside. The aim is to restrict the growth of the population on the *minifundia* without interfering with the big landlords' monopoly over land. Quite simply, a family with fewer children can more easily afford to remain on a tiny plot of land. It is no longer necessary for the entire family to sell their labour power; they need only sell a part of it, generally the man's, in order to survive. These birth control programmes promote the semi-proletarianization of the peasantry precisely because they are a response to the needs of imperialism and the local dominant classes. The process restricts the flow of proletarianized peasants towards the towns while maintaining the system of exploitation which benefits the capitalists.

Because of its ties to the land, this semi-proletariat constitutes a very elastic and very cheap industrial reserve army. The temporary emigrant sells his labour power more cheaply because his means of subsistence come from the little plot of land worked by his family. He can even survive during the periods when the capitalist no longer needs his labour. Hence this class of semi-proletarians is much more useful to the capitalists than a sub-proletariat piled up in shanty towns. Such a class is also less likely to challenge the system of exploitation since semi-proletarian semi-peasants cannot be organized so easily, scattered as they are throughout the various rural areas.

The official bodies mentioned earlier do not set out to establish education programmes about birth control. They do not try to introduce women to the idea of contraception or provide them with easy access to it. If they did, they would be doing an important job, enabling women of every social class to control their own bodies, gain some understanding of their sexuality and decide, on the basis of genuine knowledge, just how many children they wanted to have.

But of course this would be to forget that these organizations serve imperialism and the dominant classes. They only seek to impose contraception, especially permanent contraception, on women of the exploited classes. The rich can have as many children as they like. The following figures on the 'clients' of the A.P.R.O.F.E. (Association for the Well-Being of the Ecuadorian Family) birth control programme clearly illustrate who are the targets of these programmes. Since education is still the prerogative of the wealthy, it is clear that most 'clients' of these programmes are women from the impoverished classes.[6]

A.P.R.O.F.E. 'Clients'

Women with some primary education	72.8%
Women with some secondary education	22.9%
Women who have completed their secondary education	4.3%

In the Guayaquil shanty town, the *Suburbio* Battalion (a battalion of the National Army which engages in so-called development programmes) is helping with several compulsory birth control programmes, financed mainly by A.I.D. (the North American agency for financial 'aid' to developing countries).

In 1969, a programme of malaria control in operation on the coast was discovered to be just a camouflage for a massive programme of sterilization of local peasant women. In July 1974 there were several reported cases of peasant children having been castrated. In the various rural medical dispensaries throughout the country, Protestant 'missionaries' are promoting sterilization programmes in which mainly indigenous peasant women are sterilized without their consent or even knowledge. They turn up at the dispensaries, or sometimes at hospitals serving the poorer areas of the towns, to be treated for some illness (appendicitis, parasitic infections, etc.). As part of their 'treatment' the women are sterilized without even being told.

The Peace Corps was expelled from Bolivia following revelations that it was surgically sterilizing women in the Altiplano. Then in 1974 it was expelled from Peru for similar reasons and because it was deemed to have infringed upon the country's sovereignty and worked against the interests of the exploited masses. Yet in Ecuador the Peace Corps is still allowed to operate as it chooses.

These birth control programmes fit into the more general context of genocide of the poor of Ecuador. At the same time as the poor were being compulsorily sterilized, the country was thrown open to an influx of foreigners. Since 1950, the government has actively promoted the colonization of the 'uninhabited areas' of the Oriente (the area to the east of the country which includes part of Amazonia) by foreigners, especially North Americans. Throughout the 1960s and to this day, Protestant missionaries, especially the Wycliffe Bible Translators (with their Summer Language School) have established themselves in the region to 'save the souls' of the indigenous population in these 'uninhabited areas'.

In actual fact the nomadic population of the area were an obstacle to the oil companies' plans to take over these oil-rich territories. Most of the Indians were therefore herded into reserves directly supervised by the Summer Language School, where they were taught that it was 'God's will' that they leave the land to the companies.[7] The Aucas, a tribe known for its warlike disposition, was practically eliminated by a sudden epidemic of polio soon after the arrival of the missionaries in an area where oil had recently been discovered.

It is quite clear that programmes of compulsory birth control which fit into such a framework cannot be to the advantage either of the population as a whole or of the women concerned. Such programmes do nothing to raise women's consciousness or to help them control their own bodies and lives; on the contrary they are instruments of domination which help to control and destroy the exploited classes as a social force.

Whatever the arguments in favour of birth control, one cannot but condemn these programmes. The fight against them is a necessary part of the popular struggle for a just society in which people will control their own lives and in which women will really control their own bodies through freely-chosen and freely-available contraception.

Peasant Women and Popular Struggle

Because peasant women have such an important social and economic role in Ecuador, they have participated in every aspect of social life. From the time of the Conquest right up to today, peasant women have taken an active role in popular struggles, beginning with resistance to the Spanish invaders. The most famous women of this period are Baltazara Chiaza and Lorenza Avemanay, who led the Guano and Guamote Revolts in 1778 and 1803; they were both eventually executed by the Spaniards.

The most important indigenous revolt of the colonial era was led by Fernando Daquilema in 1871. His second-in-command was an indigenous woman, Manuela Leon, who played a major role in the movement. Hundreds of *criollas* and *metizos* women participated in Ecuador's struggle for independence from Spain (1802–22).[8] But independence, once achieved, brought no real change to the living conditions of most of the population, and certainly not to those of the overwhelming majority of women. The colonial economic structure had been preserved almost intact.

The struggle between the big landowners of the Sierra, who sought to maintain the pre-capitalist structures which emerged from the Spanish Conquest, and the nascent bourgeoisie of the Coast, who wanted to establish their own political hegemony, came to a climax with the 'Liberal

Revolution' of 1895 in which women played a considerable part. Women from the popular sectors joined the men in the popular armies or *montoneras* led by Eloy Alfaro. Joaquina Galarza de Larrea was even promoted to the rank of Colonel for her role in the battles of 9 April and 6 August 1895.[9] The 'Revolution' led to certain progressive legal reforms, including changes in the status of women. They were given access to public office and university education, a law on marriage did away with the Church's monopoly and made divorce possible, another law protected married women's civil rights, etc. The Liberal Constitution of 1896 established new criteria for the right to vote (one now only had to be aged over 21 and be able to read and write). Women became full citizens *de facto*, although express recognition of women's civil rights was not enshrined in the Constitution till 1928 (Article 13). Ecuador was thus the second American country, after the U.S., to give women the vote.

Throughout this century, women have continued to fight alongside the men against exploitation and oppression. There were many of them in the 15 November 1929 Movement which paralysed all economic activity in Guayaquil for a week and which was to become one of the turning points in the struggle of the working class. Tomasa Garces expressed the women's courage and willingness to fight in this strike when she and her children lay across the tracks of the railway to prevent trains strike-breaking by leaving the station. The strike ended on 15 November with an attack by the 'forces of law and order' on a demonstration by thousands of men, women and children. At least 1,500 people were killed.

Women also participated in the 1944 'May Revolution' against the dictatorship of Arroyo del Rio. Following his overthrow and replacement by Velasco Ibarra, the country enjoyed a fleeting period of freedom. The 1945 Constitution, the most liberal Ecuador has ever known, recognized the complete legal equality of men and women in marriage and the full legal independence of women. During this period, a woman became the leader of the Ecuador Workers' Confederation, one of the biggest trade unions in the country: when the Federation of Indigenous Ecuadorians (F.E.I.) was set up, a woman, Dolores Cacuango, became its first General Secretary.

Since 1936 several women's organizations have been formed. Roughly speaking, they fall into two types: (1) those which are essentially concerned with organizing well-to-do women (including women from the petty bourgeoisie) around social issues and the defence of certain 'female' demands characteristic of their class interests; and (2) those in which the participation of proletarian women is decisive, which set out to defend the interests of the people and fight for a new society. Until recently, the organization of women from the popular sectors took place practically only within mass organizations, either left-wing political parties or trade unions. There were no structures set up exclusively by these women in which they could organize relatively auonomously.

In January 1975 a *Comite Femenino de Solidaridad con los Conflictos Laborales* was set up in Quito. This Committee, which was composed of women from the popular sectors, mainly workers, and some students, emerged at a time when popular struggle was on the increase in Ecuador. Its aim was to promote and channel the popular sectors' solidarity with various struggles, especially strikes, so as to strengthen the unity of the working class. The members of the Committee explained their objectives in the first issue of their journal, *Pachacama* (named after a textile worker killed by the forces of 'law and order' during a strike in December 1974).

> This committee is made up of women because we believe that, despite the heavy exploitation women have suffered, despite the fact that they have been relegated to a secondary role and used outrageously by the enemies of the people, these same women, in the factories, in the market place, in the kitchen and in the fields, have understood that the time has come for a new stage of active participation, for unity with the demands of the people, for insistence on their rights, for protest against abuses and for struggle against their enemies. [10]

The Committee has been involved in several strike support actions, and tends to concentrate on more specifically female problems by trying to educate the people about the importance of the question of women in the class struggle. To achieve this it works with the trade unions and the husbands of women workers on strike.

Since June 1976 Women's University Brigades have been established to 'make the University serve the people'. While the various bureaucratic and/or bourgeois organizations, as well as the government, try to organize working-class women in 'women's groups' centred on their role as mothers, the Brigades aim to link up women's problems and the popular struggle. They define their task as follows: 'to develop the means necessary for analysis of the problematic of women, of the University and of the country, in order to find ways to promote women's participation and mobilization.'[11] The Brigades are already operating in the working-class districts of Quito, mainly with women employed in the construction industry, the retail trade, services and textiles.

Notes

1. The importance of agriculture in Ecuador is revealed by the following statistics. In 1974 the rural population accounted for 58.6 per cent of the total population; 46.5 per cent of the economically active population were engaged in agriculture. The Gross Domestic Product was also dominated by agricultural production:

   Gross Domestic Product (U.S. $ millions)

Sector	1970	1974
Agriculture	447	719
Manufacturing	290	518
Mining	23	256

   Source: Banco Central de Ecuador, *Ecuador en Cifras*, 1975.

2. Alain Dubly, 'Exposicion para la humanizacion de las plazas comerciales de Riobamba', *America Indigena*, Vol. XXXIII, No. 2, 1974, p. 417.
3. *Equateur, Nouvelle Strategie de l'Imperialisme: Reformisme Bourgeois et Luttes de Classes*, CEDETIM, No. 38, June 1976, p. 28.
4. The infant mortality rate is 87.3 per 1,000 inhabitants and reaches 101.3 per 1,000 in the Sierra; see Instituto Nacional de Estadistica, *Serie Estadistica, 1967–1972*, Quito, 1974.
5. CEDETIM, *op. cit.*
6. Carlos Roldan, *Penetracion Imperialista en el campo de la salud: Control de la Natalidad*, Universidad de Guayaquil, 1975, p. 98.
7. See CEDETIM, 'Les compagnies pétrolières et l'ethnocide des Indiens equatoriens', in *op. cit.* pp. 23–8.

8. See Chapter 2.
9. Ketty Romo Leroux, *Situacion Juridica y social de la mujer en el Ecuador*, Universidad de Guayaquil, 1975, p. 85.
10. *Pachacama*, No. 1, January 1975.
11. *Manifesto of the B.F.U.,* Quito, September 1976.

Mexico: Women and the Working Class

Women in the Economy

Although women participated actively in the armed struggles of 1910–21, they benefited little from the victories of the Revolution, winning not much more than the right to hold land. Peace came and the economy began to pick up, but the number of women workers still remained very small. The few who did find wage employment, however, were often very active in politics and the trade union movement.

During and after the 1939–45 War, accelerated industrialization and import substitution substantially increased the demand for labour, both male and female. The accelerated development of capitalism in Mexico from then on has particularly advantaged certain social groups so that income is increasingly concentrated in the hands of a small segment of the population. Studies in 1950 and 1969 show that the top 10 per cent of families have been the main beneficiaries; only 30 per cent of Mexican families have increased their income over the last twenty years, whilst the remaining 70 per cent have seen their living standards actually fall.[1]

Naturally working women come mainly from these poorer families. It is well known that 'in Mexico, where the distribution of income is very unequal and is becoming ever more so, the pressure of women on the labour market stems increasingly from the poorest strata.'[2] Even though economic growth makes it possible to absorb more and more women into the new dynamic sectors of industry, women continue to be concentrated in the tertiary or service sector. But the overall percentage of women in the economically active population has moved up from 4.6 per cent in 1930 to 7.4 per cent in 1940, 13.6 per cent in 1950, and 18.8 per cent in 1960, and it reached 19.2 per cent in 1970.[3] Given the inaccuracy of the agricultural statistics, these figures mainly reflect the growing numbers of women in industry and the service sector. The latest census illustrates the distribution of the economically active population.

Economically Active Population by Type of Activity and Sex, 1970 (%)

Sector		Women	Men
Agriculture		10.8	46.2
Industry		19.6	23.6
Oil	1.63		
Mining	1.15		
Manufacture	92.56		
Construction	3.66		
Electricity	0.97		
Total	*100.00*		
Services		59.8	25.2
Transport	1.17		
Services	71.55		
Government	4.65		
Commerce	22.60		
Total	*100.00*		
Miscellaneous		9.6	4.8

Source: *IX Censo General de Poblacion*, Mexico: SIC, 1971.

The structure of women's employment in Mexico is similar to that in other Latin American countries. Two-thirds of women workers are to be found in the tertiary sector, and only 20 per cent work in industry and 10.8 per cent in agriculture.

Agriculture

Many people who have analysed the census results have disputed the accuracy of the figures on agriculture and demanded improvements in the methods of data collection. The low figures for women's participation in these economic activities largely reflect the fact that women's work in the countryside is inadequately recorded,[4] since women's part-time work in the fields is not taken into account and often not even declared.[5]

Despite these reservations about the agricultural statistics, it is clear that the structural crisis in agriculture has produced a rural exodus. While both men and women are being forced to leave and head for the towns, there are more women than men amongst the migrants aged between ten and nineteen years, and, according to the 1970 census, more women than men are leaving the low-pay areas. In other words the process of migration begins with the women.[6] Once in the towns, the most frequently adopted option open to peasant women is to work as servants, living-in with their employers and working full-time, in the literal sense of the word. The alternative is to settle into the shanty town way of life which we shall deal with later. But many of the migrant women find that they cannot get a job of any sort and end up swelling the ranks of the unemployed.

Industry

Women workers in industry are concentrated in manufacturing, generally in the least modern, small or medium-size factories. These firms remain competitive by paying very low wages, which is why they take on women workers who will accept less pay than men. Out of about 500,000 women in industry in 1970, some 92.56 per cent worked in manufacturing. In some firms between half and 80 per cent of the workforce earning around 500 pesos a month is made up of women.[7] About one-third of the women in manufacturing work in clothing and about one-fifth in the food industry.

In the modern industries, women are found mainly in clerical jobs or in those final stages of the productive process which neither demand nor teach particular skills.

Tertiary Sector

The tertiary sector, which accounts for 60 per cent of Mexican women wage earners, includes: transport, administration, the retail trade, public and private services such as banking, finance and insurance, medical and hospital services, teaching, information, leisure, repairs, the hotel trade, cleaning services and domestic service. We will only deal with the most important areas.

The Retail Trade: Apart from those who work in the big urban centres, the women in this branch (22.6 per cent) tend to work part-time in small family businesses or as market stall-holders. Naturally they also have to cope with their own domestic tasks. 49 per cent of them are employees, 28 per cent are self-employed and 11 per cent work unpaid in small family businesses.

Public and Private Services: More than half the women workers in the tertiary sector are concentrated in the services proper (71.55 per cent of the sector as a whole, employing 1,058,654 women). Only 2.7 per cent of these women have completed their higher education. 33.6 per cent of posts in the liberal professions are occupied by women, whilst in education and research they account for 30.6 per cent. They form 10 per cent of the country's technical and university staff and 2.1 per cent of its management personnel.[8] 46.2 per cent of these one million working women are domestic staff employed by individual families as servants. The '*criadas*', as their employers call them, do a job which gives them no social status whatever, and 9 out of 10 get less than 500 pesos a month for doing it.[9] On top of all this, they are usually forced to provide the son of the house with his sexual initiation. Of the rest of the women wage earners in the service sector, about half work in the preparation and sale of food, the others in cleaning, housing and other services.

From the above figures, we can see that one-fifth of Mexican women wage earners work directly as servants for privileged families, while one-third of them spend their time outside the home engaged in activities which are in some way an extension of the domestic tasks traditionally assigned to women. These estimates are based on the census figures, but it is clear that, going through the list of women's occupations, the real proportions must be even higher. In industry women are concentrated in administration and in the clothing trade. Elsewhere, they work as teachers, nurses, secretaries, prostitutes, waitresses, cleaners and stall-holders. The better-off tend to own little shops selling clothes, food and millinery; a few run schools where dancing, secretarial skills, languages, yoga, etc. are taught.

Striking Inequalities

The disparity between men and women's salaries emerges clearly from the table below, and is particularly pronounced in non-agricultural activities. Almost half of all women workers earn a maximum of $40 a week; in the countryside, there is a similar kind of discrimination with twice as many women as men being 'unpaid family workers'. (Amongst the Mexican peasantry, it is customary to pay the men instead of the women.)

Economically Active Population by Sex and Monthly Income, 1970 (%)

Income Group (declared incomes in pesos)*	All Activities		Non-Agricultural Activities	
	Men	Women	Men	Women
Up to 499 pesos	44.1	47.7	18.9	45.1
500–999 pesos	27.2	26.6	35.0	27.1
1,000–1,499 pesos	12.6	13.1	20.3	14.0
1,500–2,499 pesos	8.1	8.3	13.2	8.8
2,500–4,999 pesos	5.1	3.5	8.1	3.7
5,000–9,999 pesos	1.9	0.8	3.1	0.8
10,000 pesos and over	1.0	0.6	1.4	0.5
Total	*100.0*	*100.0*	*100.0*	*100.0*

*Note: 12.50 pesos = U.S. $1.00.
Source: *IX Censo General de Poblacion*, Mexico: SIC, 1972, from tables 4 and 5 in Gloria Gonzalez Salazar, *La mujer en America latina*, Vol. 1, Mexico: Sepsetentas, 1975.

In 1970, 7.4 per cent of women were unemployed, as opposed to 2.7 per cent of men. 69.6 per cent of housewives were registered as 'inactive', doubtless a gross exaggeration hiding the real level of female unemployment.[10]

The women wage earners tend to be young. According to the table below, more than 60 per cent of active women are between 15 and 29 while 90 per cent of working men are between 20 and 60 years of age.

Women Wage Earners By Age

Age Group	12–14	15–19	20–24	25–29	30–59	60–64
% of Female Economically Active Population	5.1	20.9	24.1	17.4	15.5	14.1

Source: *IX Censo General de Poblacion*, Mexico: SIC, 1972.

Higher education is only available to a narrow section of the population in general and to an even more limited number of women. At the higher levels, it becomes more and more difficult for women to gain access. About half of the country's illiterates are women. In the primary schools the proportion of boys and girls is about even, but it begins to be unbalanced in the secondary schools and there are only about 20 per cent of girls in tertiary education. However, about two-thirds of the pupils in the so-called 'sub-professional' schools are women.[11]

Urban Women

The conditions of work in the urban centres present some interesting parallels. Although the range of jobs and social advantages are much wider than in the countryside, the rural exodus to the towns has increased the supply of labour on the market enormously. True, the towns attract a high proportion of the economically active population by providing a concentration of activities—industrial, commercial, cultural, educational, etc. But the destitution of the shanty towns presents the other side of the coin.

In Mexico City and the surrounding areas, the proportion of women in the labour force reaches 34.1 per cent; in Guadalajara, women account for 30.8 per cent of all workers and in Monterrey, 26.3 per cent.[12] In these three urban centres, the proportion of women in the economically active population far surpasses the national average, which is around 19 per cent. However, these industrial towns do not absorb the whole of the labour force which pours into them and, as a result, there is an equivalent disproportion in

Slaves of Slaves

the figures for unemployment. In Mexico City, as in other
urban centres in Latin America, the so-called informal
sector[13] is growing rapidly. A recent study concentrating on
that part of the female labour force not absorbed by the
formal sector proposes the following hypotheses: as a
woman's participation in the formal sector decreases due to
her age, so her participation in the informal sector
increases.[14] It is indeed true that older women are often
found selling papers, lottery tickets, etc.

The analysis of work in the informal sector presents
certain problems in that the census categories do not cover
every variety of this kind of work. Some activities are never
declared, others are not even included in the questionnaires,
some overlap with various types of formal work. The table
below attempts to quantify the proportion of low paid
workers and shows that 27 per cent of Mexico City's
workers earn less than the official minimum wage.

Low Paid Workers

Marginal Occupational Groups	Distribution by Sex		% Earning Less Than Official Minimum Wage		Average Monthly Income	
	Men (%)	Women (%)	Men (%)	Women (%)	Men (pesos)*	Women (pesos)*
Stallholders	59.8	40.2	50.8	79.8	1,251	907
Unskilled Workers in service sector (mainly domestic servants)	28.2	71.8	41.2	92.3	1,012	446
Unskilled Production Workers	78.3	21.7	28.1	61.1	1,109	881
Unskilled Building Workers	100.0	0.0	65.0	–	810	–
Farm Labourers	94.2	5.8	n.a.	n.a.	n.a.	n.a.

*Note: 12.50 pesos = U.S. $1.00.
Source: H. Munoz Garcia, O. de Oliveira and C. Stern,
'Migration et marginalite occupationnelle dans la ville de
Mexico' in *Espaces et Societes*, No. 3, Paris: Anthropos, July
1971, pp. 89–104, Tables 5 and 7.

One thing which emerges quite clearly is that women are concentrated in two categories, stall-holders and domestic servants, which correspond to the lowest income groups. The table also illustrates the level of sex-based wage discrimination, especially amongst unskilled production workers. The concept 'marginal occupation' roughly corresponds to work in the informal sector.

Any possibility of choosing between types of work, relation to work, access to social advantages and to education is of course determined by class position. The informal sector or marginal work performed by the working-class women of Mexico takes place either in the street or in other women's homes. Most important are living-in domestic service and the various daily- or hourly-paid jobs taken on by single mothers or married women with many children, such as washing, mending, ironing, cleaning, looking after children and the sick, and generally helping out during festivals or when the parents are away. The average daily wage of these women, who go from house to house throughout the week, is about $4.[15] If a young woman from this class is 'presentable', she may graduate to a job as salesgirl, receptionist, waitress or secretary, posts usually occupied by women from a different class. As for the older women, to whom such avenues of advancement are closed, they are found selling food, fruit, newspapers and trinkets, either from stalls or their homes.

The Indian women in Mexico City are also forced into this position: they sell fruit, sweets and craft products, and often suffer police persecution for 'not having a street trader's licence'.[16] There is undeniably a racist element to this discrimination in employment—as in other Latin American countries, the Indian women are at the very bottom of the social pyramid.

Also the marginalization of poor and elderly women in Mexico City is quite evident. One of the authors of the report mentioned above concludes that it is mainly lack of opportunity for work in the formal sector, especially as far as women over thirty are concerned, which leads them to become 'incorporated into informal sector activities within which they create a specific demand for their services'.[17] The table below shows the extent to which migrant women are marginalized.

Proportion of People in Marginal Occupational Groups, by
Sex and Migrant Grouping (%)

Sex	Recent Migrants	Intermediary Migrants	Older Migrants	Natives by Adoption	Natives by Birth
Men	27.1	19.5	16.7	13.8	14.5
Women	64.0	45.4	34.7	25.2	19.3

Source: Munoz, Oliveira and Stern, *op. cit.,* p. 102.

Apart from a university-educated minority, petty-
bourgeois Mexican women tend to 'believe that it is
undesirable to work outside the home; the prevailing social
norms tell them that their place is in the home and that
their children, their dignity and their respectability will
suffer if they have to seek outside work.'[18] For the working
class, on the other hand, women like men have to work in
order to survive—they have no alternative. The difficulties
experienced by poorer women in finding work are often
explained in terms of a supposed lack of demand for
women's labour. In both cases the dominant ideology is
clearly operating.[19] The division of society into classes has
become generalized under industrial capitalism; the con-
comitant exclusion of women from production in the
formal sector now takes the particularly intolerable form of
a 'weak demand for women's labour', hiding the fact that
women are being forced into long hours of work both at
home and outside, and are being excluded from so-called
intensive labour (requiring a higher level of skill and
intellectual concentration in exchange for shorter working
hours and better pay). Naturally 'if class society is to
survive, it is crucial that women should not put *all* their
energy into social production; some of their strength must
be kept for their activities in the home.'[20]

When their husbands' salaries are not sufficient to meet
the family's needs, petty-bourgeois women also begin to
work. They start at home, baking cakes, embroidering,
knitting, sewing, giving private tuition and making toys,
dolls, boxes, artificial flowers, etc. Some find jobs in the
outside world in small shops, in food stores, chemists and
restaurants. There are also special schools where gymnastics,
dance, yoga and 'personal development' are taught; both

the teaching staff and the clientele are almost always women.[21]

Work and Fertility

It has long been thought that having many children was one of the factors which prevented women from working. Yet this obviously does not apply to single mothers who are their families' only providers and, according to the 1970 census, 12 per cent of all families in Mexico fall into this category. The argument fails in other ways: for instance, a study carried out in 1966–67, dealing only with married women, found that women working at home had, on average, 5.1 surviving children. The corresponding figure for women working outside the home was 4.1, and 4.7 for those who had no paid employment.[22] A subsequent enquiry[23] disclosed that working women had, on average, more children than those who stayed at home. Economic need *forces* these women to work. The idea that children prevent women from working thus clearly expresses an ideological class position. Politicians may argue as loud as they like that women cannot work because of children but the fact remains—the correlation between work and fertility is that the women with most children *have* to work.[24]

Unionization

Only a small proportion of wage-earning women in Mexico are unionized; as a result they are relatively powerless to demand better working conditions and fairer wages, to fight against unemployment or to resist discrimination. We have no figures for the number of women who are union members but it must be low since only 22.5 per cent of all workers are unionized. Bearing in mind that 7.6 per cent of union members work in agriculture, 33 per cent in trade and services, and 59 per cent in industry, it is clear that the number of women in these unions must be very small since women are concentrated in the least unionized sectors, agriculture and services.[25] And even those women who are unionized are not represented in proportion to their numbers.[26] One might add that, since the corruption of the trade union leaders has often meant that workers' demands are blocked or dropped, it is not surprising that, when it comes to women workers, the union leaders sometimes even contribute to the level of exploitation. To take a few examples:

> In about 95 per cent of firms within the Federal District, the state labour laws are broken; the employees, most of whom are women, get less than the official minimum wage, no overtime pay, and are not registered for social security. There are practically no unions for these workers. In the bigger firms, the unions often side with the bosses, or have a purely nominal existence.[27]

> The employees in the *cocinas economicas, taquerias* and *cafe de chinos* (working men's cafes), most of whom are women, get less than the minimum wage, are not registered for social security and . . . do not even enjoy the most elementary privileges . . . In these often under-capitalized enterprises, the bosses frequently react to a strike by closing the place down.[28]

> The seamstresses are traditionally one of the most exploited sectors in Mexico . . . in practically every case, they receive less than the official minimum, even though they usually have to work between 10 and 12 hours a day.[29]

> Thousands of women and children seamstresses, most of whom work from home, are exploited in a completely unregulated way. They are paid from 15 to 20 cents for sewing shirt collars and from 5 to 7 pesos for sewing trousers.[30]

In any case, given the unions' timidity, the inadequate representation of women workers and the abundant supply of labour, laws passed to protect women workers are used by the bosses to force them to accept derisory wages or simply as an excuse not to employ women at all. For instance, in response to the law which stipulates that a creche be provided once a certain number of women are employed, many employers simply refuse to employ that number of women. And the law which prevents employers forcing women to do night-work is used as an excuse for paying them lower wages.

Production and Reproduction

In conclusion, one can say that the way the capitalist system in Mexico allows women to enter production is such that they get pushed into those activities which are social extensions of housework. 'Few of the country's women wage earners are industrial workers . . . production belongs to the men; the women's role is secondary and, from an economic point of view, dependent.'[31] This role determines the type of social participation open to women and the resulting precariousness of their economic position. In factories they are mainly employed as clerks or cleaners; elsewhere they usually occupy subordinate posts requiring little initiative and offering no prospect of promotion. It is particularly hard for a woman to secure one of the better paid jobs or to rise in the hierarchy.[32] The ones who do succeed are assimilated by the system and offer no challenge to the established authorities—on the contrary, they are only too pleased to accept the privileges associated with their status.

On top of all the strictly economic factors, the society's ideological superstructure contributes decisively to the oppression and exploitation of women at work. Nearly all the authors we have quoted refer to it in one way or another. Within a sexually differentiated labour market, the supply of and demand for women's labour is largely determined by the role society has traditionally ascribed to women, a role which implies their subordination to men. Women's access to salaried work is limited by their function as mothers and by their legal status. Traditional values ensure that women who work in the outside world are made to feel guilty while cultural attitudes influence the sort of education they receive. The unequal development of Mexico makes it impossible for women to obtain paid employment on a massive scale, but even the few who do find such work are exposed to the pressure of the dominant values. Women's participation in work is determined by ideological and social factors as well as by purely economic ones, especially when it comes to the sexual division of labour and to women's own attitudes towards work.

In evolving the most amenable system of recruiting labour, capitalism has developed an ideology and a set of values which help to keep women oppressed *even when* they participate in the productive process.[33]

Notes

1. Ifigenia Navarrete, *La distribucion del ingreso en Mexico, tendencias y perspectivas*, Mexico: UNAM, 1964; *El perfil de Mexico in 1980*, Mexico: Siglo XXI, 1971. The 1969 figures are from the I.B.R.D. Report on Mexico, Washington, 1971.
2. Teresa Rendon and Mercedes Pedrero, *La mujer trabajadora*, Mexico: Cuadernos de la Secretaria del Trabajo, 1975, p. 16.
3. Gloria Gonzalez Salazar, 'La participacion de la mujer en la actividad laboral de Mexico' in *La Mujer en America latina*, Vol. I, Mexico: Sepsetentas, 1975, pp. 108, 111, 134.
4. Lourdes Arizpe, 'Woman in the informal labour sector in Mexico City: a case of unemployment or voluntary choice?', paper given at the *Women and Development Conference*, Wellesley, Mass.: 2–6 June 1976, p. 12.
5. Gonzalez Salazar, *op. cit.,* p. 16.
6. Rafael Ruiz Harrell, *Aspectos demograficos, educativos y laborales de la mujer en Mexico, 1900–1975.*
7. Till 31 August 1976, 12.50 pesos = $1. Since then, the currency has been devalued and has fluctuated widely. Minimum values as follows:

1 September 1976	1 $ = 19.50 pesos
26 October 1976	1 $ = 26.50 pesos
22 November 1976	1 $ = 28.48 pesos
11 December 1976	1 $ = 20.50 pesos
20 January 1976	1 $ = 22.50 pesos

8. Gonzalez Salazar, *op. cit.,* pp. 118, 119.
9. Rendon and Pedrero, *op. cit.,* p. 16 (12.50 pesos = $1).
10. Mercedes Oliveira, 'La opresion de la mujer en el sistema capitalista', *Historia y Sociedad*, No. 6, Mexico: Segunda Epoca, 1975, p. 5. Percentages correspond to declared unemployment.
11. S.E.P., 'Participation de la mujer en el sistema educativo en Mexico', appendix to 'Educacion y promocion de la mujer', Mexico: Sepsetentas, 1975, No. 227.
12. S.I.C., Direccion General de Estadistica, 'Encuesta nacional de hogares', quoted in 'Situacion de la mujer . . .', p. 44.
13. The I.L.O. characterizes the informal sector as follows: 1) ease of access and flexibility in the creation of new

employment; 2) operates outside of social and labour legislation; 3) low productivity, small-scale production, rudimentary technology; 4) low salaries, low income. See OIT-PREALC, *La mujer y el empleo en America latina*, Geneva: 1976, p. 16.
14. Arizpe, *op. cit.,* p. 15.
15. *Ibid.,* passim, especially p. 26.
16. *Ibid.,* pp. 24–29. See also his *Indigenas en la ciudad de Mexico, el caso de Las Marias*, Mexico: Sepsetentas, 1975, No. 182.
17. *Ibid.,* p. 39.
18. *Ibid.,* p. 22.
19. I.L.O., *op. cit.,* pp. 7–9.
20. I. Larguia and J. Dumoulin, 'Aspectos de la condicion laboral de la mujer' in *Casa de las Americas*, Havana: 1975, No. 88, pp. 45–60.
21. Arizpe, *op. cit.,* pp. 23–4.
22. I.M.E. 'Investigacion de la familia en Mexico', quoted by Maria del Carmen Elu de Lenero, 'Trabajo de la mujer y fecundidad' in *La mujer en America latina*, Vol. I, Mexico: Sepsetentas 1975, pp. 55–84.
23. Guadalupe Zetina, 'El trabajo de la mujer casada y su vida familiar ante el cambio social', thesis, Universidad Ibero-americana, 1972, quoted in Elu de Lenero, *op. cit.,* p. 75.
24. Elu de Lenero, *op. cit., passim*.
25. Gonzalez Salazar, *op. cit.,* p. 122.
26. Rendon and Pedrero, *op. cit.,* p. 16.
27. Statement by the Women's Action Secretary of the *Federacion de Trabajadores del Distrito Federal* (C.T.M.) to the newspaper *El Dia*, 25 March 1973, quoted in Gonzalez Salazar, *op. cit.,* p. 114.
28. Statement by the General Secretary of the *Union Sindical de Trabajadoras de Cafes, Restaurantes, Pastelerias y Similares* of the Federal District (Mexico City and suburbs) to *El Dia*, 21 February 1973, quoted in Gonzalez Salazar, *op. cit.,* p. 123.
29. Statement by the workers' representative of C.T.M. Section 9 to *El Dia*, 27 January 1973, quoted in Gonzalez Salazar, *op. cit.,* p. 123 (1 peso = 8 cents at the time).
30. Oliveira, *op. cit.,* p. 5.
31. Gonzalez Salazar, *op. cit.,* pp. 115–6.
32. See Rendon and Pedrero, *op. cit.,* p. 7, Diaz, *op. cit.,* p. 21, Elu de Lenero, *op. cit.,* p. 67, Gonzalez, *op. cit.,* p. 111, Arizpe, *op. cit.,* p. 14, Oliveira, *op. cit.,* pp. 5–9, Larguia, *op. cit.,* p. 55; see also *Ano internacional*, pp. 51–52.

Puerto Rico: Women, Culture and Colonialism

Arise, arise, sister in poverty, cast off
despondency and prepare to fight, to fight
for your freedom.[1]
Juan S. Morcano*

A Cultural Mosaic and Female Subjection

Puerto Rican society is the very patriarchal product of the
fusion and confusion of Spanish, African and indigenous
Indian culture. Its short history has been marked by two
separate colonial periods. *Machismo*, which defines women as
everything men are not, was introduced through Spanish
colonization (1493–1898) and has remained a lasting
inheritance—women are defined as mothers, wives, house-
keepers, 'weak and fragile' creatures to be protected. Later,
under U.S. domination beginning in 1898, the differences
between men and women imposed by tradition were
exploited even more intensely, as we shall see.

Spanish colonialism built up a whole mythology around
women. They were taught that their universe should be
confined to the home, and were brought up amidst a clutter
of domestic utensils, the symbols of their future life.[1] Their
whole being was shaped to revolve around men, that
admirable sex whose natural social environment, the street,
was so much broader. The femininity demanded of women
required them to be gentle, passive, submissive, faithful,
pure and docile. The higher a woman's social and economic
position, the more she was expected to display these
characteristics. Women were inculcated with this machist
conception right from childhood, not only by what they saw

---

*'Paginas Rojas' (1919), quoted by A.G. Quintero in *Lucha Obrera
en Puerto Rico*, 2nd edition, CEREP, San Juan, Puerto Rico, 1972.

and heard at home but also in school and through the games they played.

Within Puerto Rican society other myths were enthusiastically developed, such as that of the old maid, the self-sacrificing mother, the devoted wife, all centred around the idea of chastity. The Church was in a privileged position to transmit the ideology of the dominant class, reinforcing the institution of marriage and consolidating the family as the cornerstone of society. The ideal of the 'Virgin' Mary functioned as a form of psychological blackmail, by forcing women to take upon themselves all the repression and self-contempt implicit in the religious dogma. Indeed Puerto Rican society still distinguishes between 'pure' women ('Virgin' Marys) and 'loose' women or prostitutes.

In Puerto Rico, marriage is like a Yagrumo leaf.[2] On the one side, it is presented as the means of self-fulfilment; on the other, it is a trap snapping shut on many who had thereby hoped to escape social and family oppression. Mothers today have learnt from what they have suffered and often insist that their daughters acquire professional skills so that they can get a job if necessary, for instance if they get divorced, or their husband falls ill or economic conditions deteriorate.[3] The increasing importance attached to women's education in contemporary Puerto Rico has not dispelled the idea, however, that women are better off looking after the children. The home remains the proper place for a woman.

While Catholicism certainly played an important role during the period of Spanish colonialism, Protestant doctrine was equally virulent later under the U.S. occupation. Protestantism was used to intensify the submissiveness and enslavement of both men and women, shifting the emphasis from the ideal of the 'Virgin' Mary to an all-powerful omnipresent male God. Religion came to condition every aspect of life, from the way people dressed and combed their hair to the way they spoke, who their friends were and what they liked.

We have been describing the historical process which has influenced Puerto Rican women—but who are these women we are talking about? Puerto Rican historical writings contain little reference to the role of women. Occasionally individuals are alluded to, or passing comments

are made about the pastimes and general idleness of the
white women who came from Spain as wives or prostitutes
to set up home or to service the garrison on San Juan Island.
In any case, as white women they were privileged compared
to the Tains or Africans whom the historiographers never
refer to as women, only as slaves. Equally, during the 19th
Century, the accounts only deal with women from the land-
owning class whose literary and artistic activities did, it is
true, enrich *one aspect* of our cultural heritage. But hardly any
mention is made of the 60,000 women workers employed as
servants (18,453), washerwomen (16,855), seamstresses
(5,785) or factory hands (3,910).[4]

U.S. Domination

One cannot separate the situation of Puerto Rican women
from the political and economic realities of the country. In
1898 Puerto Rico was invaded by the U.S. Army and for 78
years it has been the promised land for capitalist interests
from the colonial metropole. During the first 40 years of
military rule, the country was economically transformed.
When the invaders arrived, women's participation in the
economy was essentially limited to the agricultural sector,
their emancipation held back by precarious conditions of
employment and limited access to education. Few women
managed to get even a primary education (1,387 in 1899)
and nearly all stayed at home (82 per cent).[5] Then, as
business enterprise developed, so did the need for cheap
labour. By the beginning of the 20th Century, the military
regime had launched an extensive education policy and
women's participation in the economy increased, rising to
9.9 per cent in 1899 and 26.1 per cent in 1930.[6]
   At the time of the invasion, Puerto Rico was an
agricultural country, with an economic structure unsuited to
the needs of North American capitalist interests. The first
stage of the country's new phase of colonization involved a
disarticulation of the agrarian and social structures: the
haciendas[7] were replaced by *plantaciones*.[8] To achieve this, the
government introduced measures forcing the *hacendados* to
sell their lands. Puerto Rico was integrated into the
protected North American market, its currency devalued,

credits blocked, etc. The *hacendados* emigrated to the cities
and gradually took up liberal professions. A commercial
bourgeoisie grew up around the *plantaciones* and the peasants
became wage labourers.

For the women of the bourgeoisie, a minority of whom
had in the past struggled to gain access to education, there
were considerable benefits to be had from the military
regime's education policies. Women increasingly became
'professionalized' and in so doing they helped to support the
dominant ideology and gradually adopted the cultural values
of the new colonial system imposed by the United States.
Teaching became one of the main professions for bourgeois
women. In 1930, 74.5 per cent of all teachers were women,
compared with only 30 per cent in 1899.[9]

Working-class women's living conditions were also
changing. As they became integrated into manufacturing
industry, they began to break away from the traditional
structure which cast them as helpmates to the men. They
were mainly employed in the clothing industry (as home
workers initially), in craft workshops and in the tobacco and
cigarette factories.[10] Contemporary accounts detail their
precarious working conditions and the desperately low
salaries they were paid.[11] While the bourgeois women united
to fight for the right to vote, Puerto Rico's working-class
women set about creating trade unions to demand better
wages and working conditions. By 1904 women's trade
unions were already active and men began to consider
women as comrades in working-class struggle.[12]

The 1930s marked a new stage in Puerto Rico's colonial
history. Unlike the women of their class who had found
many opportunities in the field of education, the second
generation *hacendado* men were squeezed by an economic
crisis engendered by the new colonial system. Their
response was to establish a class alliance with a section of
the agrarian workers and evolve a radical populist ideology
based on nationalism, embodied in the new Popular
Democratic Party which won the 1940 elections. There
followed the first attempts to industrialize the island and a
second economic transformation was soon under way.
Puerto Rico broke with the political and agrarian
colonialism represented by the North American sugar
companies and moved towards commercial and industrial

colonialism. The new economic structure, along with the repercussions of the Second World War,[13] massive emigration to the U.S. and the repressive anti-working class Taft-Hartley Act, which banned strikes and controlled industrial relations, contributed to the disintegration of the Puerto Rican proletariat.

A programme of economic and social development was launched and did succeed in raising the standard of living, the number of jobs, wages and other indices of social well-being. At the same time it introduced a variety of myths, including equality of opportunity, the self-made man, social mobility and the meritocracy. Industrialization, initially light industry, especially clothing and electrical goods, was protected under the country's new political status as an Associated Free State (1952). What this really meant was that the country effectively remained a colony but was allowed an apparently democratically elected government which could be manipulated by U.S. metropolitan interests.

In the last 30 years, the process of industrialization has increasingly moved towards highly specialized heavy industry such as refining, chemicals, petrochemicals, etc.

Consequences for Women

Despite all these changes, women's position has not improved one jot. In fact new mechanisms of domination have emerged, making the struggle for women's liberation in Puerto Rico even harder. The development of education and new employment opportunities have apparently broadened women's participation in the work force. But to return to our original question, what women are we talking about? The effects of the 'welfare state' and the myths of social mobility so current in North American sociology have had a considerable impact. 'Professionalized' bourgeois and petty-bourgeois women have indeed gained access to new types of work. But women from the working class are finding it more difficult to get new jobs while government policy is to encourage them to put all their hopes in their children—hence the great stress on education.

Women represent 24 per cent of the work force in Puerto Rico today. Their participation has actually fallen since

1930, when the figure was 26.1 per cent. This is partly due
to the decline of the clothing industry during the 1960s, the
drop in demand for domestic servants, and the increase in
the level and duration of schooling.[14] Women are still the
preferred work force in manufacturing industry, accounting
for three-fifths (57.2 per cent) of all employees in this sector
in 1971.[15]

In 1970, 67 per cent of Puerto Rican women workers were
employed in private industry and 33 per cent were state
employees.[16] Almost half (46 per cent) of all government
employees were women and at the lowest levels of the
public sector hierarchy, even more women than men are
employed. But the higher up one goes, the fewer women
one finds, until at the top levels of industrial management,
the professions and business, women are conspicuously
absent. In descending order, the jobs most frequently held
by women are factory hand, office clerk, doctor or lawyer
and technician. A majority of women work in the tertiary
sector.

Discriminatory recruitment policies reflect employers'
stereotyped attitude towards women. The allocation of
certain jobs to women goes hand in hand with the notions of
'feminine qualities' used to debar women from night work
or work which involves lifting and carrying heavy objects.
Yet technical progress should make nonsense of such
attitudes and broaden women's employment possibilities.
Enquiries into women's marital status during job interviews
constitute another form of discrimination, especially for
pregnant women who find it very difficult to secure
employment of any sort. A third type of discriminatory
practice appears under the cloak of labour legislation,
including laws which determine the age at which a woman
can start working and what sort of jobs she can do.

A more serious kind of discrimination is exemplified by a
recent report which states that 'women's unemployment is
not necessarily a cause of poverty or great human suffering
since in most cases it is not the head of the family who is
affected. Consequently, it is right that male employment
should be given priority in the development of public
policy.'[17] This in a country where 51 per cent of women
heads of family are wage earners and nonetheless find it
impossible to escape poverty.[18]

Given this state of affairs, it is understandable that Puerto Rican women's participation in the workers' movement has declined. According to the 1972 Guide to Labour Organizations,[19] only 34 of the 502 union leaders are women. Only 2 of these 34 are respectively President and International Representative of their unions; there are 46 men occupying equivalent positions. The 32 remaining women are in charge of various union sections, a position occupied by 424 men. Attempts have been made to explain this situation away by suggesting that Puerto Rican women are especially committed to their homes and husbands, and that their husbands' tacit or verbal consent is thus a precondition for any action they might undertake. Such an explanation is fairly feeble, especially considering the very active participation of women in the workers' movement at the beginning of the century. As we have pointed out, the situation faced by Puerto Rican women cannot be divorced from the political and economic realities they experience. Even though social structures have been affected by the recent economic changes, women are still seen in traditional terms. When women go out into the world to get a job, they take on an additional burden and still have to cope with their 'family and domestic responsibilities'. Mothers do not have access to the sort of facilities which would enable them to go out to work freely; family and couple relationships are still affected and altered whenever women work outside the home.

To compound the double burden borne by working women, there is the impact of the myth of the 'self-made man/woman'. The education system and the mass media constantly stress that it is only through individual effort and aptitude that one can rise in the social hierarchy. Taught to compete frantically against one another, workers are unlikely to develop any collective solution to their problems, or to grasp the real causes of their difficulties. Demands are simply diverted towards inappropriate goals.

So the fact that women's work often provides important additional revenue for their families can sometimes reinforce oppression, by making women hesitant to express discontent about their working conditions. The effect of such fears in preventing women from developing their class consciousness was compounded by the exposure of the venality of trade union leaders in the 1930s.[20] Many men and women still think of the unions as corrupt and useless institutions run for the benefit of union officials rather than for the rank and file. This is gradually changing, however, as working-class organization in Puerto Rico revives.

Just as in other Latin American countries (except Cuba, since the victory of the Revolution), women in Puerto Rico are cast as sex objects, things to be consumed. The mass media present women as parasites who ride on the backs of men and have no real sense of responsibility. Advertising depicts them as pleasure objects whose whole universe revolves around men.

Demographic Policy: An Instrument of Subordination

Sterilization is another very important aspect of institutionalized oppression. Puerto Rico today has one of the world's highest rates of sterilization. There are about 600,000 women of childbearing age (14–49) in the country, two-thirds of whom use some form of contraception. The government has launched a campaign aimed at the 212,000 women who still practice no birth control of any kind. According to Antonio Silva Iglecia,[21] the Under-Secretary for Health charged with family planning, the aim of the programme is to introduce the underprivileged to the birth control methods already available to the privileged. A recent Report on Employment, Education and Training presented to the Governor of the Associated Free State in 1973[22] puts the matter rather more bluntly, stating that, in order to reduce the level of unemployment (which is officially at 29 per cent, affecting 192,000 people), it is necessary to reduce the growth of the working-class sector of the population.

Campaigns for birth control were first launched in Puerto Rico in 1925. At first, the population at large remained indifferent to the campaigns, although they were vigorously attacked by the various religious groups in the country. These first family planning programmes were in fact developed by groups of 'prominent' citizens, not by the government, who did not step in until 1940 when it set up 122 contraception clinics in rural medical centres and village public health units. But there was still considerable

139

resistance to the idea from health officials so the family
planning programme, which was not officially a government
service, was hardly promoted at all.

Various studies show that in 1947–48 surgical sterilization
as a method of birth control was known but not used to any
great extent. At the time, only 6.9 per cent of women of
childbearing age had been sterilized.[23] But in 1949 the
government began to put much more stress on sterilization
as a means to limit demographic growth and intensified its
campaign; by the end of the year the figure for married
women of childbearing age who had been sterilized had
reached 16.5 per cent.[24]

In 1954 the Puerto Rican Association for Family Welfare
appeared on the scene. The Association was affiliated to the
International Federation of Family Planning and was
financed both by the (U.S.) Federal Government and by the
Government of the Associated Free State (i.e. Puerto Rico).
Its aims were to inform people about the population
problem and family planning, as well as to carry out
scientific research into the efficacy and acceptability of
various contraceptive methods.

It thus came about that, right from 1956, Puerto Rican
women (along with the women of Mexico and Haiti) were
used as guinea pigs in the first tests on the contraceptive
pill. During these experiments, which involved hormonal
vaccines and intra-uterine coils as well as pills, the women
patients were given no protection against side effects, and
some of them died.

Nor were women given any information about sterilization
and the risks involved in the operation. No mention was
made of the fact that it was irreversible and might well have
unpleasant side-effects. On the contrary, they were told that
it was the ideal and most economical solution to their
problems. No options were presented; the women were kept
totally ignorant of alternative methods of contraception and
of the health care they should have been receiving from
their doctors.

The present population policies must be seen in the
context of the prevailing political process. During the 1930s
the country's social contradictions sharpened. A strong,
nationalist movement with a mass following threatened to
pull the island out of the U.S. orbit. Capitalist interests were

forced to protect themselves by seeking to control any possible future public uprisings. Later, between 1940 and 1950, Puerto Rico was transformed economically, in keeping with its new political status *vis-à-vis* the U.S. It was thus essential to co-ordinate demographic growth with the island's economic development if capitalist exploitation was to continue.

The Family Planning Programme only really got going in the 1960s. Around 1965, the Programme was given considerable support by the U.S. President and Congress. Robert MacNamara openly declared that family planning had proved less costly than any other kind of development programme.[25] The Family Planning Programme was extended and other social welfare programmes substantially cut. In other words, the North American capitalist interests had realized that effective command of a country's demographic growth was a useful means of controlling any crises which might arise out of the system of exploitation set up by the multinationals.

During this period the Puerto Rico Department of Health and Social Welfare carried out a study of the links between sterilization and cancer of the uterus. It was only then that it emerged that one-third of all women aged between twenty and forty-nine years had been sterilized, a figure confirmed in a study carried out by Dr. Vasquez Calzada in 1968, which stated that 35.5 per cent of women had been sterilized.[26] According to Dr. Calzada, two-thirds of the sterilizations were carried out when the women involved were between twenty and twenty-nine years old, and 92 per cent before they were thirty-five. This means that Puerto Rican women are sterilized at a younger average age than almost anywhere else in the world. Also, according to Calzada, the incidence of sterilization as a method of birth control correlates negatively with the level of education of the women concerned.

The massive sterilization of Puerto Rican women was recently further confirmed in a study by Saul Pratts, who notes that in 1975 36.4 per cent of Puerto Rican married women of child-bearing age had been sterilized.[27] Pratts' study shows that sterilization is most common amongst women aged over thirty-five, other methods being more common amongst younger women. The pill emerges as the most commonly used method of contraception in Puerto Rico today. According to Pratts, sterilization is most common in the shanty towns where 35 per cent of his sample had been sterilized. Those living in council accommodation were less likely to have been sterilized (26.5 per cent of married women).

The study also brings out the two main reasons for sterilization given by the majority of women Pratts interviewed. Medical reasons accounted for 50.9 per cent of answers, and the desire not to have any more children for a further 32.7 per cent. But many of these women also said that they now regretted not being able to have children or that they had suffered complications as a result of the operation. Some said that their marital life had suffered either because of a cooling sexual ardour or because the operation had led to misunderstandings and sometimes to divorce.

In 1974 and 1975, a further 11,600 people in Puerto Rico were sterilized. Sterilization of men is also on the increase, despite a certain resistance. Ten women have been sterilized for every man. According to Dr. A. R. Silva Iglecia, the number of sterilizations has dropped thanks to the recent promotion of alternative methods under the Family Planning Programme. This confirms that the main reason Puerto Rican women opted for sterilization in the past was that they were unaware of other types of contraception.

The fact that women now have access to alternative methods does not mean that they are no longer being manipulated. The propaganda for the birth control programme has concentrated on arguments about poverty and overpopulation (347 inhabitants per square kilometre in an area of 8,896 square kilometres). Pseudo-scientific justifications by the authorities include the exhaustion of agricultural resources, overcrowding and increasing pollution. Finally, the authorities have tried to show that rising unemployment, cuts in public services and the aggravation of various social problems were all due to demographic growth. Behind all this propaganda lies the fact that Puerto Rico is going through a new stage in its economic transformation, as it moves towards a highly specialized form of industrialization requiring high investment and a low labour input. The problem of co-ordinating demographic growth with dependent economic development has re-emerged in a new form.

Puerto Rico does not really have a population policy; the government presents migration, the high birth rate and the low mortality rate as the main factors determining high population density. To justify its present policies, the government contrasts the high birth rate with the low mortality rate and argues that zero population growth is essential in order to maintain an 'optimum social and economic equilibrium'. Control of overpopulation and overcrowding are now the main planks of the government's platform—the possibility of a more equitable distribution of income and available resources is never referred to.[28]

Nobody mentions the fact that over the last fourteen years (1960–74) the natural population growth rate has *fallen* by 40 per cent: in 1974 the rate was 13.5 per 1,000 inhabitants, compared to 25.5 per 1,000 in 1960. Nor does anybody bother to point out that one of the reasons the population of Puerto Rico is rising is foreign immigration.[29]

We are not trying to deny the importance and necessity of a population policy in Puerto Rico. On the contrary, we are saying that no such policy actually exists. The government's 'population policy' amounts to little more than blaming demographic growth for all the problems caused by colonial exploitation and economic and political dependence. The underlying meaning of this Family Planning Programme becomes apparent when one examines the manifest attitudes of government officials and the historical and economic evolution of the country. At a meeting of the Society of U.S. Government Economists held in Puerto Rico, the administrator of the Office of Economic Development, Teodoro Mascoso, said: 'As for me, I'd pour contraceptives into the island's drinking water and insist that one man in three undergo a vasectomy.'[30]

In conclusion, it is worth repeating that the liberation of Puerto Rican women is not simply a matter of female emancipation. This is only the first stage; women must insert themselves into the broader arena, side by side with their male comrades, in the fight for national liberation and the construction of a socialist society.

143

Notes

1. Jorge Gissi, *Mitologia de la femeneidad*, Santiago de Chile: Ceren, 1971, pp. 168 ff.
2. Yagrumo (Yagruma or Yaruma)—a tree found in the mountains of Puerto Rico. Its main characteristic is that its leaves are green on top, white underneath. Hypocrites are often called 'as two-faced as the Yagrumo'.
3. Statistics provided by the Justice Department indicate that in the financial year 1974-75, there were 35,362 applications for divorce, 16,209 of which were carried over from the previous year. 60 per cent (21,533) of the applications were considered, 12,888 accepted and 8,645 either rejected, filed, dropped or deferred. 13,829 were left pending. The 12,888 cases accepted represent an average of 1,074 divorces a month, as against 2,600 marriages a month, one divorce for every 2.5 marriages. Over the last 6 years 68,822 divorces were granted, affecting 78,330 children, of whom 67,744 were less than 18 years old at the time.
4. Isabel Pico, 'The Struggle for Women's Equality in Puerto Rico: The Historical Experience', speech delivered at the second annual meeting of the *National Conference of Puerto Rican Women*, New York City, 29 June 1974, p. 3.
5. *Ibid.*
6. *Ibid.* The figures quoted do not cover women's participation in agricultural work.
7. *Hacienda*—in Latin America, a house surrounded by farmland.
8. *Plantaciones*—cash crop plantation. In Puerto Rico, these plantations were owned by North American firms based in the metropole and represented on the island by Puerto Rican administrators.
9. Pico, *op. cit.,* p. 4.
10. In the tobacco industry, many women were employed to strip the tobacco leaves.
11. Angel Quinto Rivera, *Lucha obrera en Puerto Rico*, Puerto Rico: CEREP, 1972, 2nd ed., pp. 35, 66–7.
12. See Chapter Two of this book.
13. Demobilized soldiers drawn mainly from the proletariat of the plantations. A Veterans Administration was set up after the Second World War to provide loans, study facilities and mortgages, effectively separating them from their original social group and imbuing them with new values.
14. Isabel Pico, 'Estudio sobre el empleo de la mujer en Puerto Rico', paper presented at the *Conference on Women and Development* held in Mexico, 14–19 June 1975, p. 10.
15. Estado Libre y Asociado, Comision de Derechos Civiles, *La igualdad de derechos a deberes de la mujer puertoriquena*, San Juan, p. 133.
16. Isabel Pico and Marcia Rivera, 'Datos basicos sobre la mujer en la fuerza obrera en Puerto Rico' in *La mujer en America*

latina, Vol. II, Mexico: Sepsetentas, 1975, p. 116.

17. Comision de Derechos Civiles, *op. cit.,* p. 196.
18. Pico and Rivera, *op. cit.*; Estado Libre Asociado, 'Comision para el mejoramiento de los derechos de la mujer', p. 5 (xerox). In 1970, 47.6 per cent of working women were divorcees (Population Census, 1970, U.S. Dept. of Trade); one should also bear in mind the 26.8 per cent of working women with 'absent husbands'. The distinction between 'divorced' and 'absent husbands' is by no means clear, since it is difficult to tell whether the husband is absent because he holds a job outside the island or because he has deserted his wife. Nevertheless, the figures give a clear indication of the number of homes in which the head of the family is a woman.
19. Comision de Derechos Civiles, *op. cit.,* p. 134.
20. See Helene Icken Safa, 'Conciencia de clase entre las trabajadoras latinoamericanas: un estudio de casos en Puerto Rico' in *La mujer en America Latina*, Vol. 1, Mexico: Sepsetentas, 1975, pp. 166–98.
21. Wilda Rodriguez, '11 mil esterilizados en dos anos', *El Nuevo Dia*, 8 March 1976, p. 3.
22. 'Sterilization Abuse of Women: The Facts', Health/P.A.C. Bulletin No. 62, January-February 1975.
23. Jose L. Vasquez Calzada, *La esterilizacion femenina en Puerto Rico*, Puerto Rico: U.P.R. Recinto de Ciencias Medicas, escuela de Salud Publica, Depto. de Epidemiologia, Bioestadistica, Ciencias Sociales y Demografia, April 1973.
24. *Ibid.*
25. Bonnie Mass, 'The Political Economy of Population Control in Latin America' in *Women in the Struggle for Liberation*, W.S.C.F. Book, Vol. III, No. 2/3, p. 29.
26. *Ibid.* This study used the same basic sample as the Puerto Rico Department of Health.
27. Saul J. Pratts Ponce de Leon, *La esterilisacion femenina en los sectores pobres de Puerto Rico*, unpublished, Rio Piedras, Puerto Rico, June 1975. The author used the sample of poor families selected by Professor Miguel Valencia which was also used in a 1974 study directed by Dr. Nieves Falcon on the effectiveness of various poverty programmes.
28. In 1966, North American companies established in Puerto Rico made $281 million in profits. In 1970 they imported $583.9 million and in 1974 they repatriated some $1,300 million. One might say that Puerto Ricans produce a great deal of wealth which they never see again.
29. Saul Pratts' study of female sterilization in the poor sectors of Puerto Rico includes the following table on the place of birth of the inhabitants of Puerto Rico, based on the 1960 and 1970 population censuses (Pratts, *op. cit.,* p. 19):

Inhabitants of Puerto Rico by Place of Birth

Place of Birth	1960 Total	%	1970 Total	%
U.S.	49,092	2.1	106,602	4.0
Overseas U.S.	3,024	0.1	27,835	1.0
Other Countries	10,224	0.4	52,792	1.9
Foreign Ascendancy	—	—	43,130	1.6
Puerto Rico	2,287,200	97.3	2,432,828	91.5
Total	*2,349,540*	*100*	*2,712,033*	*100*

The table shows a 15.4 per cent increase in the population from 1960 to 1970. 60 per cent of these 362,493 people were born abroad, mainly in the U.S. and the U.S. overseas territories. One other significant factor has been the high rate of immigration by refugees from Cuba—there were 1,000 Cuban immigrants in 1960, as opposed to 33,000 in 1970.

30. Miguel Santin, 'Perspectiva: Asi cualquiera . . .', *El Nuevo Dia*, 24 April 1976, p. 19.

El Salvador: Super-Exploitation and Super-Oppression

The text below is made up of long extracts from an account of the situation of women in El Salvador. It was proposed to us by a woman who wishes to remain anonymous. The text allows us to glimpse the level of exploitation and often appalling conditions under which most women live in that country. For obvious reasons we have not reproduced the names of the individuals quoted. (Additional Note by the Publisher: This piece was of course written before the successful Sandanista Revolution of 1980.)

The young girl in the mini-dress, her silhouette outlined by the bluish light spilling from the room behind her, leans against the bars which line the window, her hips shaking mechanically in time with the strident rock music coming out of an adjoining room where other women sit on wooden chairs and wait impassively for their next customer. Her face is an anonymous blob glimpsed as we move slowly forwards along the poorly lit street lined by one storey houses (*torchis*). Her movements are stereotyped, almost inhuman; one might even believe she was a marionette, struggling clumsily to free herself from the enormous spider's web into which she has stumbled.

My guide, a social worker, tells me that she is most likely a peasant woman driven in search of work to San Salvador by hunger or the needs of a large family.

> She probably went to school for three or four years and then had to drop her studies in order to help her mother with the domestic chores, cultivating their little plot of land and looking after younger brothers and sisters. If she was lucky, she will have got a job as a maid with a well-to-do family, but as you can see, she is quite good-looking, so she probably had

the misfortune to attract the attentions of the husband or one of the sons. [My guide shrugged his shoulders.] How could she have resisted? She needed to work. What is more, *machismo* is an institution here. Everybody knows that, in El Salvador, most upper class men begin their sexual education with one of the family servants or with a local prostitute. It is the traditional rite of passage from childhood to adolescence. The rest of the story is no doubt equally banal: the mistress of the house realized what was going on and indignantly threw the girl out for having dared to sully her home, and as far as the family was concerned, that was the end of the story. As for the girl, she had no references and did not know how to do anything apart from wash clothes and clean floors. She has been 'marked', so nobody will want to marry her; her only way out was what we've just seen.

Prostitutes like her charge 20 cents a trick. An eleven year old virgin can be bought for 4 dollars. In many coffee plantations in the interior, the *jus primus noctis* still prevails; it is considered quite normal for the planter or one of his sons to deflower a little peasant girl when she reaches puberty. The last population census shows that a third of fourteen year old girls have been pregnant at least once.

The scene changes. I am sitting on the edge of an iron bed in a little room at the end of an empty corridor in the Chalchuapa Health Centre. My interlocutor, Dr. V.A.G., is a woman doctor on night duty; she sits opposite me on the only chair.

'I worked in the country for a few years, about 26 kilometres from Santa Ana, and I was always coming across little girls of two or three months with serious vaginal infections. At first I thought it must be due to a parasite, but I was wrong. I began to question the mothers. The peasant women are very taciturn on the subject and it takes time to win their confidence. After several months, one of them gave me the true explanation. She told me that it was fairly common to remove a new-born infant's "virtue".'

'What does that involve?' I asked.

'Taking a razor blade and cutting a little cross, just there,' she answered, without naming the clitoris more specifically.

'Why?'

'So that later, they will work harder and stay away from men longer.'

Perhaps this custom has been handed down through the ages from the days of the Mayas and Pipils, but that does not explain why it has survived right up to the end of the 20th Century. The real reason is clearly the fact that most of the peasants of El Salvador are illiterate and live a precarious and marginal existence, excluded from the socio-economic system in every way, except for occasional stints of badly-paid work as coffee pickers.

El Salvador is a tiny country (the Tom Thumb of America, as Gabriela Mistral once put it), with a population of 4,200,000 people living piled one on top of the other in a mountainous and volcanic area covering a mere 21,000 square kilometres. The country's G.N.P. increases annually by about 3.5 per cent, whilst the rate of population growth is 3.7 per cent.

Although the annual *per capita* income did move up from $245 in 1969 to $290 in 1973, the increase was almost entirely due to industrial development in the urban centres, especially in San Salvador, where the average daily income was already as high as $1.54 in 1971. In the countryside, however, the average income remained virtually static between 1951 and 1971; despite gradual inflation during those twenty years it only went up from 36 to 37 cents a day. The rate of unemployment was around 5 per cent in 1961. Ten years later it was oscillating between 14 and 22 per cent, according to the criteria used.

Little girls do worst in the struggle to get a place in primary and secondary school, and are even more disadvantaged when it comes to University. After all, they are destined to be mothers, and the best preparation for that task is not to fill their heads with nonsense out of books but to take them out of school as early as possible in order to help their mothers with the housework and looking after the small children.

According to one of my informants who comes from the interior and whose job involves her in the rural areas, the attitude of the male peasants also contributes to the high percentage of girls who drop out of school. The men adopt a protective attitude towards the girls in their family and believe that the best place for them is where their mother can keep an eye on them. This conservative and patriarchal attitude is also responsible for the high percentage of early marriages in the countryside, where many fathers marry off their daughters at thirteen or fourteen. The girls go straight from their father's hands into their husband's, like ignorant little slaves who are not even granted the privilege of choosing the Christian names of their numerous offspring.

Another problem which weighs heavily upon the women of El Salvador is the prevailing mediaeval conception of marriage. A man who has slept with a girl will boast about his conquest to his friends, to boost his male self-image. In doing so he ruins the girl's reputation and destroys her hopes of finding a husband. And of course he himself will adhere to the dominant morality and will lose all respect for the girl. He will certainly never consider marrying her.

> The cinema, the TV, the international magazines all portray a modern and open attitude towards sexual morality which is very much at odds with the rigid and conformist behaviour expected of people in our society. An inexperienced young girl who has been influenced by these international norms may well succumb to her fiance's pressure. Women's virginity is one of the most difficult problems for women who want to liberate themselves. Ever since our childhood we have been told that we will not be able to get married if we do not preserve our virginity. There is a terrible stigma attached to loss of virginity and a young woman who is not a virgin may never be able to establish a stable relationship with a man. If it is known that a girl is not a virgin, everybody will look down on her and nearly all the men who approach her will do so with 'bad intentions'. The existing double morality is a very heavy burden, borne entirely by the women.

According to the last census 26.8 per cent of women in El Salvador are married, while 26.4 per cent live with a man in some less formal union. Unmarried mothers may be deserted at any moment, in which case the father usually ceases to contribute anything at all to his children's upkeep. Faced with such circumstances, women have very few options. They can establish a precarious union with another man, find a job as a factory worker or servant providing somebody is willing to look after their children, or they can become prostitutes.

'And what sort of life do the peasant women lead?' The doctor answered with a bitter smile:

> Their life is terrible. The average peasant woman gets up at 3.30 or 4 in the morning to light the fire for cooking the maize. Then she pounds it on a stone, feeds the animals, prepares the meal and washes the clothes. At midday, she takes most of the meal to her husband and while he eats, she ploughs the fields or wields a scythe and generally carries on with whatever her husband was doing. Afterwards she goes home, feeds the children and eats what little is left. Then she goes to fetch water and feeds the animals again. She is probably beaten, frequently pregnant and suffers many miscarriages.

This is the usual fate of peasant women. One of them, N.M.G., was born in the interior. Her father was the foreman of a small coffee plantation. At sixteen, she went to San Salvador to continue her studies, much against her family's wishes. For years she lived with her uncle and worked nights as a washerwoman in a hospital in order to keep herself while she studied to become a secretary. Twenty years ago, she got a job as a teacher, but she still carried on with her studies. Today she is a voluntary supervisor in a peasant co-operative sponsored by the Church. Theoretically she gets a salary of $80 a month but in practice the co-operative is short of money and for three years she has received nothing and has to cultivate a little plot of land in order to feed herself and her children.

'Peasant children now have more access to education,' my informant continued, 'many of them get through six or seven years of primary schooling. In my day, very few got through to the end of the third year, and qualifying as a secretary was about as difficult as getting a university degree is today.'

The education statistics reflect this general improvement, although 40.5 per cent of the population is still illiterate. Only 44 per cent of children go to school, and peasant children are particularly disadvantaged. In the urban areas 47.2 per cent of school-age children have received some formal education, whilst in the countryside only 28.5 per cent of children have ever seen the inside of a schoolroom.

'One of the few ways that a young peasant girl can get a decent education is to become a nun', N. explained to me. 'The Church will help them to get trained as a nurse or as a teacher, but then it sends them to the towns to work in a Catholic school and they spend the rest of their life educating the children of the rich who can afford a private college. None of these women ever return to work in the countryside, where they are so desperately needed.'

While I was riding through San Salvador from Ilopango Airport, the driver took a certain pride in pointing out the modern factories, the new North American style commercial centre, the banks and the office blocks on the outskirts of the town. We headed for the residential areas where the rich live (Colonia San Benito, Colonia Escalon, etc.) and I was surprised to see how much they had grown in fourteen years. They now stretched all the way to the slopes of the volcano, less than a mile from the crater itself. The prosperity of these areas was evident. But the centre of San Salvador was very much as I remembered it, overcrowded, falling to bits, full of houses with corrugated iron roofs.

As we left the residential areas I caught a glimpse of the shanty towns—rows and rows of cardboard shacks with palm frond roofs, naked children with swollen bellies, women carrying pitchers of water on their heads, unemployed men and teenagers whose only activity is at night, when they slip into the city to commit robberies and muggings.

We pass Santa Tecla, El Congo, Coatepeque and finally reach my village, Santa Ana, which has deteriorated even more since my last visit. The shanty towns have spread and now surround the town. They grow so much faster than the public housing schemes sponsored by the government or the Church. 'Nothing ever happens here,' I tell myself again and again, during the few weeks I spent there. The apparently prosperous capital is surrounded by the swaying greenery of coffee and sugar plantations, by cotton fields and a growing army of underpaid peasants who bring in the harvest.

Forty-four years ago, the Great Depression provoked a peasant revolt which spread throughout the country and which was drowned in blood by the dictator Maximiliano

Hernandez Martinez. Ever since, an almost constant succession of military regimes has imposed an unstable equilibrium, but what efforts there are to improve the education system, to provide decent houses for the poor, to raise salaries to an acceptable minimum remain grossly inadequate.

In Europe I had been asked if there were any liberated women in my country. I set about looking for some, and was surprised to find quite a few women who had overcome the barriers of male social prejudice and had secured a good education and jobs which offered some chance of personal fulfilment. The second surprise was that nearly all the women I talked to were engaged in some sort of social task and were fighting against the apathy, hostility and resistance of the authorities in an effort to help the poorest sectors of the country. A few examples come to mind immediately, for instance the woman doctor mentioned earlier:

I worked for a few years with the Maryknoll project in Villanell. There were no doctors there so I set up a mobile clinic. The only water supply was a river polluted with human excrement and effluent from a coffee processing plant. All the fish had died and the women had to push aside lumps of excrement and rotting coffee pulp to fill their pitchers. They gave this water to their children without even boiling it. I tried to open a permanent clinic but I failed. People did not trust me. They only began to trust me when I started living like them, in huts with floors of beaten earth, sharing the same food as them and going everywhere in blue jeans with a bag of medicines and medical instruments slung over my back. I established a mutual aid health scheme; each family which registered paid 10 cents a month and 40 cents per consultation. Those who were not registered had to pay 80 cents. I taught them to keep rudimentary accounts, to watch the stock and to ask for the drugs we were running out of. In less than four years we had a pharmacy worth at least $4,000, and it was managed by the peasants themselves.

'What happened to the programme?'

I was watched right from the start. When things began to work really well, the families who were working with me

153

started to get into trouble; one of their sons would be arrested for stealing a cow, that sort of thing. The accusations were always false, of course, but what could we do? Eventually I had to recognize that I was doing more harm than good to those who were helping me, so I dropped the whole thing and came to Chalchuapa.

The case of G.B. is also illuminating. G. worked as a secretary in an office and in the evening she helped with an aid programme for teenagers. After a while, she became involved in the Maryknoll popular housing project in Santa Ana, interviewing applicants for houses built by the future occupiers on their days off or in their spare time. G. organized talks for the women, taught them to live in a house with running water, electricity and a lavatory, and helped to form groups of workers into efficient co-operative units.

'And what happened?'

'My superior, Father I., called me in one day to inform me that I was being transferred to Sonsonate. I asked him why, given that I lived in Santa Ana. He said that there had been complaints about my lifestyle. My sister and I live together and the priest said that the neighbours had complained about noisy parties, people coming in and out, music late at night, etc. I told him that my sister and I lived perfectly normally and that in any case it had nothing to do with my work. The next day a delegation of families who had already built their houses and a group from the Peasant League came to see him and he agreed to their demand that I should stay in Santa Ana, but that very evening he fired me.'

'Why?'

G. shrugged. 'Pressure from above. Somebody in the government probably. I was suspect because I had been very active in voluntary social work, and because I wanted to help poor families.'

I also met three young women who are about to complete their medical studies at San Salvador University. C.S.P., A.E.F. and M.R.P. are exceptions amongst the mass of generally apathetic women in San Salvador. C.'s father is a Professor of Medicine at the University. Two of the girls have brothers who are doctors. When they are not studying, the three spend their weekends doing voluntary work as interns in the Chalchuapa Health Centre. After studying in the well-equipped University Medical Centre, they were all horrified by the absence of the most elementary hygiene, the shortage of basic drugs and the complete lack of comfort in the Health Centre.

'The flies are terrible,' says A., 'there is a coffee processing plant next door which is a breeding ground for flies and we do not even have enough money to buy grilles for the windows of the surgery.'

They all wanted to work amongst the peasants in the outlying areas, but they were not given permission to do so.

'Do many of your fellow students apply for this kind of work?'

'Some, not many. Women mainly. Few of the men students have any time for idealism. They are too busy trying to get their diploma so they can earn a lot of money. They would not want to go and work in some backwater. It is usually the women who embark on medical studies as part of an ideal. The men do it to provide a comfortable life for themselves. Furthermore, it is practically impossible for students with any sort of left-wing ideas to practise in the countryside. They are very closely watched and obstacles are constantly put in their path. The authorities are frightened that they might get involved in political activity and show the peasants what is going on.'

One more example of the official inertia which suffocates the efforts of specific groups who try and make the life of the poor in El Salvador more tolerable: this time, my guide is an upper-class lady who has collaborated extensively with the Church in projects ranging from prison reform to care of malnourished children.

'In Santa Ana we launched a prison reform programme. The first thing we had to do was to get the director of the prison sacked. He was taking money from prisoners, who were already practically destitute. If a prisoner wanted a camp bed, a blanket or a bit more food, he had to pay for it.

'We formed a committee elected by the prisoners themselves to run the prison and apply a few fundamental reforms. They did not choose the most educated inmates as their representatives, far from it. They chose the hardest and most experienced, the ones who really knew the rules of the game. Doctor G. helped us set up a clinic, and came twice a week to look after the prisoners and their families.

'You may know what life in prison is like, but you cannot imagine what the prisoners' families were going through. When the husbands go to prison, there is no more money coming in and the women have to find some way of feeding themselves and their children. They become outcasts, because the man is in prison. Even if they have money, nobody will serve them in the market. And when it comes to finding a job, nobody is willing to trust the wife of a condemned man. On top of all this, there is the psychological torment of the conjugal visits. On Saturday mornings, the women form a queue and they are all searched, in case they try to bring something in. Then they are allowed into the cells. Imagine what it must be like: there are thirty to forty men to a cell. All they are allowed is a blanket to curtain off the bed. And there are prostitutes too.'

'Prostitutes are allowed in?'

'It is difficult to tell them from the others. Almost none of the women who come to the prison are legally married, they live with their men informally and sometimes prostitution is their job anyway. The pimp gives them from $2 to $4 to go to the prison and afterwards he collects $1 from all the prisoners who have gone to bed with them. Obviously, in such conditions, love and tenderness are out of the question. The women are treated like animals. Often the husbands are jealous, because while they are in prison they cannot keep an eye on their wives. Most of the women are horribly traumatized by the whole thing. We asked the nuns of the Assumption to help the prisoners' wives by looking after the children while the women went to the prison for the conjugal visits.'

'And what happened to the reform programme?'

'We managed to set up a clinic, a recreation room and workshops, we even managed to organize dances. But the prison doctor felt insulted. He had got used to lining up the prisoners in two rows, those with stomach problems and those with breathing problems, so that he could hand out just two types of pill. Later a new director was appointed who decided to solve the prostitution problem by admitting only married women. The prisoners went on strike.'

'And what happened?'

'The government was not at all pleased that everything had come out into the open. For the first time, people realized just how horrible prison conditions were. In the end, the prisoners won a 10 per cent increase in their food rations, the conjugal visits went on as before and trusted prisoners were let out on parole for contract work, but the committee, the clinic and all the rest were dropped. The precedent was too dangerous.'

During the few weeks I spent in El Salvador, I only saw a tiny part of the life of the society there, but what I did see was sad and discouraging. Women are second-class citizens, peasants are third-class citizens. Some people within the government are working for change, but nothing else is tolerated apart from a few closely watched groups working under the auspices of the Church.

Uruguay: Barbarism Triumphant

The position in which Uruguayan women find themselves today is one of the most dramatic in all Latin America, and probably the most tragic in the country's history. Uruguay is situated on the Atlantic coast by the Rio de la Plata, bordering on Argentina and Brazil. Until just after the Second World War it was an economically prosperous liberal democracy, which was often described as 'Latin America's Switzerland'. Yet the last three decades have been marked by an economic crisis which has gone hand in hand with a rapid deterioration of national institutions. The power structure is evolving relentlessly towards fascism.

On 27 June 1973 the military seized power and set up a puppet presidency which would be merely ludicrous were it not for the fact that the present regime is in practice one of the most brutal and repressive in all Latin America, as is amply borne out by reports from various international bodies over the last two years [1976 and 1977].[1]

'Latin America's Switzerland' has become a 'silent Chile'. National sovereignty has been systematically undermined in the process of imperialism's gradual alienation of the entire country—Uruguay has sunk lower and lower under fascism's repeated offensives.

A Little Country with a Big Myth

Uruguay first emerged as a modern state with a high level of social integration and institutional stability during the early 20th Century. The middle classes were then very much on the ascendant and many fundamental trade union rights and social demands were won.

The leading figure of the period was Battle y Ordonez, who did a great deal to stimulate the liberal economy, partly through nationalization of essential services such as the energy supply, the ports, transport, credit, insurance and the oil refineries, and partly by developing labour legislation and providing a system of social security for vast sectors of the urban proletariat. This 'Battlist' era, during which the state directed the evolution of the country's social and political life and controlled capitalist investment, was closely linked to an expanding economy. The state's intervention was decisive for the growth of employment and the redistribution of resources to disadvantaged groups, and the end result was the creation of a domestic market and the development of nascent industry.

These factors determined the country's image, both at home and abroad, as an exceptional place to live in and as an example to the rest of Latin America. Thanks to a few years of profound change, Uruguay seemed to have broken away from a past dominated by pillage, extermination, dependency and conflict.

> After nearly 30 years of superficial harmony, secular progressive Uruguay had become a metaphor for the good life. It was the country where perfection had been achieved without crisis, where stable institutions combined to form an enviable and stimulating whole. It was the country of social justice, a myth shored up with increasing desperation by a mass of well-intentioned laws. It was the country of ultra-liberal legislation, offering political asylum to all, so unlike the horrors of today. It was the country of free and compulsory secular education, of the separation between Church and State, a country which held no political prisoners (another myth which was cruelly exposed in 1933 and has now broken down completely). It seemed as if it were almost contingent that this paragon was situated in America and had an American destiny. In short, Uruguay was a country in which institutional epiphenomena were presented as the essence of social life, a country which believed that structural crises, the class struggle and conflicts of interest could be resolved simply by changing laws and Constitutions.[2]

Early Women's Victories

This society, which was capable of integrating successive
waves of European immigration, did not conceal its feeling
of superiority towards the confusion and violence prevalent
in the rest of the continent. Uruguay was a place apart, in
which women could organize successful feminist movements
and win important reforms.

Many areas of cultural and political activity were opened
up to women, who soon held important positions in the
country's administrative and professional sectors. The
precocious establishment of a Women's University in 1913
exemplifies how quickly the state could respond to and even
anticipate popular demands. Various laws were passed by
Parliament in response to the rise of feminism: in 1911
divorce on certain specified grounds was legalized and after
1913 women could get a divorce on demand. Women's
suffrage was first proposed in 1917, enacted in 1932 and
exercised for the first time in the 1938 elections. Paid
maternity leave was established in 1934, as was a law on
minors which broke with the tradition of complete paternal
authority. In 1946 a Civil Rights law established the concept
of joint parental responsibility.

The 1963 census showed that 70 per cent of the
population lived in towns of over 10,000 inhabitants,
reflecting an exodus towards the cities which has in fact led
to rural depopulation. Uruguay is thus unusual in that 80
per cent of the population is urban and 45 per cent is
concentrated in the capital, Montevideo.

Forty per cent of women between twenty and twenty-five
are economically active; 30 per cent of the thirty-five to
forty-four year age group and 24 per cent of the forty-five to
fifty-four year olds are also active participants in the
economic life of the country.

Because of the high level of urbanization, it is easy to fall
into the trap of generalizing about women's economic
activity in a way which ignores the desperate conditions
experienced by peasant and poorer women: the very fact
that these women constitute a minority actually exacerbates
the brutal segregation imposed upon them, their complete
isolation from technical or literary training, their social and
cultural restriction compared to men from the same sectors

and the severe discrimination against them in the work hierarchy. For all that Uruguayan women enjoy greater civil rights than they would in other Latin American countries, they are nonetheless still the victims of an economic, social and familial segregation which no superficial reading of the statistics can make clear.

Crisis and the Coup

The crisis which broke out in the mid-1950s was first signalled by a levelling off of livestock production. The whole process rested essentially on the agrarian structure which provided most of the country's wealth, a structure dominated by stock-rearing (wool, meat, leather) and on the domination of a small number of latifundist landlords.[3] The country's economy was, and still is, fundamentally dependent and limited. When rural technology did not improve and the conservatism of the landlords prevented any scientific application of research into animal and crop production, agriculture began to get bogged down.

The combination of population growth and the dominant agrarian class's resistance to change made crisis inevitable. Faced with such a situation, the local bourgeoisie and the traditional political parties proved incapable of providing a solution; their only answer took the form of increased dependency on international monopolies, growing subordination to the private national banking groups and deeper foreign indebtedness. As this subordination grew, the local bourgeoisie consolidated itself by incorporating the bankers who served the foreign monopolies into an alliance with the traditional big landowners.

Tortuous and contradictory as it was, the transition from democratic euphoria to present-day conditions concretized itself very quickly and became suddenly clear in the collapse of the economy in the 1960s and 70s—inflation soared to above 100 per cent in 1968 and repressive policies began to dominate the life of the country.

The particular steps on the road to fascism could be pinpointed quite specifically. For instance, 'state security measures' were enforced for 39 of the 48 months of Pacheco Areco's Presidency, measures which included a ban on strikes by state employees, a ban on trade union meetings and propaganda, closure of trade union branches and expropriation of union assets. The intensification of repression was marked by the assassination of three students, Liber Aree, Susana Pintos and Hugo de los Santos.

But these years also saw a major mass mobilization of the workers' movement, culminating in the creation of the C.N.T. (*Confederacion Nacional de Trabajadores*, the National Workers Confederation) and in united student and working-class participation in the struggle. During 1968 more than 7,000 strikes paralysed the country.

During the same decade the M.L.N. (National Liberation Movement)—the *Tupamaros*—launched an urban guerrilla campaign based on such spectacular acts as 'expropriating' banks, exposing economic fraud, and kidnapping various economic and political personalities. Women played a considerable role at all levels in the *Tupamaros*, including the leadership.

The 1971 elections took place in an atmosphere of unprecedented violence. One of the parties canvassing for votes was the *Frente Amplio*, a coalition of progressive forces and left-wing parties which represented a tremendous spirit of hope and enjoyed enormous support in the capital, Montevideo. After the election many parties denounced the results as crooked and distorted: the victor who emerged from these machinations was Jose Maria Bordaberry, who was later to endorse the June 1973 coup from the President's chair.

The dictatorship eliminated Parliament, dissolved the parties of the left and instituted a regime of terror and repression aimed at eradicating all democracy. Uruguayan women soon felt the effects of the fascist military takeover—they were exposed to ideological persecution, imprisonment, torture, hostage taking and expulsion from the country. The impact could not but be perceived politically by women at every level, in the family, individually, and in terms of trade union activity. Women were hit hard by the government's economic failures, by soaring inflation and unemployment, by currency deval-uations and sudden drops in purchasing power.

To take just one example, the new regime eliminated one of the pension rights embodied in the so-called 'Mother

Law', a measure passed early in this century guaranteeing the right of women with young children to a pension after 10 years' service.

A few indications as to the economic and social situation:

—Foreign indebtedness *per capita* is the highest in the world, equivalent to half the country's annual production ($1,500 million).

—A foreign investments law has resulted in many banks and businesses being taken over by foreign concerns.

—Unemployment in Montevideo now affects 10 per cent of the economically active population.

—Thousands of people have had to emigrate for political or economic reasons. About 500,000 people out of a total population of 2.8 million have left the country.

—Fifty-five per cent of the national budget is now made over to the armed forces and the police.

The democratic rights guaranteed by the Constitution are regularly and systematically violated while democratic institutions such as Parliament and the political parties have simply been eliminated. The military have taken over the administration of justice. Freedom of expression is virtually non-existent—everything is censored, including the press, the television, the publishing houses, authors and novelists, the cinema and the theatre. The military has even carried its war against culture into the universities and other branches of education, which have all been militarized.[4]

Trade Unions Smashed

It was not long before the repressive policy directed against trade unionism culminated in the banning of the whole C.N.T. and the persecution of its leaders. Thousands of trade unionists were fired and arrested, local branches were occupied and their assets confiscated, student union activity was banned.

The struggle against the dictatorship has already claimed its martyrs. Nibya Sabalsajaray, an F.E.U.U. leader, was arrested in her home following a day of protest against the dictatorship, and then barbarically tortured for at least 24 hours till she died, on 29 June 1974, in an infantry barracks. She was twenty-three, the daughter of a poor family, but who had managed to become a teacher.

In November 1975 the I.L.O. officially approved a Report on allegations of repression against the trade union movement taking place in Uruguay since June 1973. The Report condemned the dissolution of the C.N.T. and the unions as well as the procedure adopted by the military courts following the arrest of leading unionists. The SUNCA (National Construction Workers Union), for instance, was dissolved on 11 October 1974 by a decree which not only closed the union's offices but also confiscated its assets and stripped it of its legal identity. Later, these offices were turned into a prison and torture centre by the Montevideo Police's Grenadier Corps. The National Teachers Federation was also dissolved.

The I.L.O. resolution points out that 'the dissolutions were announced as security measures, thereby eliminating any right of appeal.' The Report also condemns mass sackings in the transport, textile and metallurgical industries, as well as in newspaper publishing. On education, the Report indicates that 'apart from the sackings, we have heard that, in 1974, 400 teachers and lecturers were hauled before boards of inquiry and suspended. In the University, some people were sacked by being retired early or by not having their contracts renewed.'

Culture Destroyed

Following the 1973 coup, an attempt by the University to intervene led to the arrest and imprisonment of its authorities. Higher education institutes such as the I.M.S. and the I.N. were closed and militarization of education became the order of the day. Representatives of the Armed Forces were installed in the most senior posts, directly under the Minister of Culture, and the three branches of education (primary, secondary and university) were placed under military directorates.

Each school was directly attached to the nearest barracks, with headmasters required to inform the corresponding military authorities about any irregularities in the school's day-to-day operation. The University was particularly affected and every faculty suffered. Certain courses were eliminated altogether; those that survived were only given intermittently. Whole institutes were dismantled. Some of the new teachers had no academic background. Scientific research was done away with altogether. Civil, mechanical and electrical engineering and mathematics were removed from the engineering curriculum. Sixty-seven per cent of the lecturers were sacked. The technical assistance these institutes provided to public and private industry, a programme which had been running since 1914, was terminated. In the Agronomy Faculty, the three experimental branches (livestock production, farm and citrus production and forestry) were paralysed, and 87 per cent of the staff resigned or were sacked. The entire staff of the Institute of Economics, that section of the Faculty of Economics concerned with gathering statistics and analysing economic data, were made redundant. The Social Science Institute, attached to the Law Faculty, was closed. In 1975, 45 per cent of the teaching and research posts in the Architecture Faculty were left vacant. The Applied Climatology section was closed outright. The lecturers of the Institutes of History, Philosophy, History of Ideas, Philosophy of History, Uruguayan Literature, etc. were all thrown out. The havoc wrought by this repression upon the cultural life of the country, striking at every level of education, and on the country's development grows ever more extensive and will take years to repair.

In the primary and secondary schools, the 'new order' trains pupils to inform on their fellows. Essay subjects include 'My parent's opinions' and 'What I think of the police'. Staff trade unionism is subject to persecution and teachers are forced to transmit the regime's political and social ideology. The fact that all University lecturers and administrative staff have to swear to abide by a so-called Declaration of Democratic Faith is yet a further indication of the prevailing level of repression.[5]

Under the provisions of Circular No. 1376/975/AH, issued by the Director of Secondary Schooling, all schools must secure the approval of the Schoolbooks Commission before any text can be used in class. Private as well as public and University libraries are subject to the book-burning policies of the regime. The military and the police regularly break in, unannounced and without a warrant, to

confiscate and destroy technical and humanist books which
have been deemed subversive. Over the last two years, over
500,000 volumes have been burnt, including works on
sociology, economics, history, art, paediatrics, etc. The
stocks of the E.P.U. and Anteo bookshops were seized,
loaded into Army lorries and taken off to be pulped. The
library of the Lithuanian Centre (18,000 volumes) was
burnt in the courtyard of the building. The works of
Uruguayan authors such as J.C. Onetti, Amorin, M.
Benedetti, F. Espinola, Vilarino and J.J. Morosoli have
disappeared from the shelves of the country's libraries.
Foreign authors banned include A.A. Machado, F. Garcia
Lorca, P. Neruda, B. Brecht, J. Ramon Jimenez. The
classics of Marxism are obviously proscribed, and perhaps
more curiously, so are the writings of Sigmund Freud.

Popular music, which in recent years had flourished in
new directions, has also been blighted: the works of
Uruguayan song writers such as A. Zitarrosa, los Olimarenos,
D. Viglietti were banned, as were the songs of many
foreigners including J.M. Serrat, M. Sosa and J. Cafrune.

Concepcion Zorrilla, an excellent actress, famous both in
Uruguay and in Argentina, was declared censored and
forbidden from entering the country. After one popular
and critically acclaimed showing of *Andes por los fuegos*, its
star, the Argentinian actress I. Ledesma, was told to get out
of Montevideo and the play was banned. Cultural
repression struck particularly hard when it closed the
independent *El Galpon* theatre group and confiscated its
playhouse. The group had been going for 27 years; its
theatre, seating 600 spectators, was considered to be one of
the best and most modern in the country. The regime's
press began by presenting the group as an agent of
international subversion, then the authorities imprisoned
many of its leading figures and stole the theatre's files.
Eventually, on 7 May 1976 a decree was issued dissolving *El
Galpon*, closing its premises and confiscating its assets—all
this despite the fact that the group is respected throughout
Latin America and had recently [1974] completed a tour of
Venezuela and Colombia which attracted international
acclaim.

Uruguay Today

The following declarations, press communiques and accounts bear witness to the regime's ferocity:

> There are more than 7,000 political prisoners in a country of less than 2.8 million inhabitants. More than 1,500 of them have been imprisoned since mid-October 1975. They are tortured night and day, constantly or intermittently, physically and mentally. They are blindfolded at all times, mercilessly beaten, forced to remain standing with limbs extended, kept without food or water; electric shocks are applied to the most sensitive parts of their bodies; they are also burnt, suffocated, stretched over sharpened iron bars . . . The women (especially the younger ones) and some of the men are kept naked for weeks and many have been raped, in some cases by trained animals . . . They are tortured individually, collectively, in front of their parents, etc. . . . (Interview with R. Arismendy published in *Casa*, March 1976, by Casa de Las Americas)

> Mr. President: Uruguay, once the Switzerland of Latin America, has now become the continent's hellhole. In 1975 we invested about $10 million in military aid to Uruguay and $7.7 million in economic aid through the A.I.D. programme. The blood of the tortured prisoners is on our hands. (Official Acts of the U.S. Congress, 25 March 1976)

> I have witnessed the most appalling atrocities inflicted on women in front of other prisoners. Some of these women had been detained in order to find out where their husbands, fathers or sons were. In other words, they themselves were not charged with anything. (Letter from a Uruguayan Army officer published in several newspapers and broadcast on the radio and television services, March–April, 1976)

The International Democratic Federation of Women condemned the repression launched by the Uruguayan military regime against the country's democrats and patriots. The Federation sent messages detailing its accusations to Kurt Waldheim, U.N. Secretary-General and

167

to Pope Paul VI. The Federation, which has affiliated groups the world over, revealed that Silvana Saldana, a young Uruguayan, died in Uruguay's prisons following the tortures she had endured (*Prensa Latina*—Berlin, 23 August 1976). Silvana Saldana was born in Salto Province. She was 28, a student in the University's School of Social Work and a militant member of the Communist Party. She was arrested by the Montevideo Joint Forces in February 1976 and savagely tortured for months. Witnesses who saw her in the barracks where she was held said that the torturers were particularly hard with her because she refused to talk. She gave only her name. In mid June she died but the dictatorship covered up the event and took her body to a shop in Ciudad Vieja (the port district of Montevideo) where she used to work: the manager refused to accept the body so it was taken to the province where she was born (Montevideo, August 1976).

In the September 1975 issue of its magazine (No. 26), the International Union for the Protection of Children denounced the disappearance of Amaral Garcia Hernandez, a Uruguayan child:

> Everybody knows that certain regimes in Latin America have institutionalized torture. What is less well known is that in order to extract confessions from people, their children are tortured in front of them. The methods used are unbelievably horrible . . . Amaral Garcia Hernandes, a three-year-old Uruguayan child, was arrested with his parents in Argentina. A few days later the parents' bodies were found in Montevideo; the whereabouts of the child remain a mystery. (*Revue Internationale de l'Enfant*—UIPE)

Deportations are also common. On 5 November 1975, pharmaceutical chemist Sonia Bialous de Dutrenit, a leading personality in the women's democratic movement, was expelled from the country. She was born in Argentina but had lived, studied, worked and brought up her family in Uruguay.

Kidnappings are another regular feature. The mother of Antonio Bacchi, a U.T.E. trade union leader, was arrested and kept hooded for 72 hours because the forces of repression could not find her son. Mrs. Bacchi is 80 years

old. Between May 1972 and October 1976, dozens of
Uruguayans were tortured to death. Many militants have
disappeared and fourteen of the bodies found in the Rio de
la Plata are still unidentified. One thousand five hundred
left-wing militants were arrested in a series of raids
launched between late 1975 and early 1976. Many of them
were tortured to death in various barracks in the capital
and in the interior.[6]

The situation in Uruguay today, though extreme, is
unfortunately not unique, especially in Latin America. Most
of the peoples of Latin America today endure savage
repression; fascist dictatorships are no longer the exception—Chile, Argentina, Bolivia, San Salvador, Haiti,
Guatemala . . .

Implications for the Women's Movement

Uruguayan women are fully aware that these conditions
determine the struggle which the people must wage against
their main enemies, the fascist government and imperialism.
The women's struggle is inseparable from that of the
people as a whole. Under such conditions, the oppression
of women as women is secondary. Exploitation and fascism
are the main determinants and only once fascism has been
rooted out will it be possible to fight for women's
liberation. The struggle demands greater social participation
and better political organization. This can best be achieved
in sectors where women play an important role, such as
education, social work, medicine and dentistry, as well as
amongst the urban proletariat.

The struggle for women's emancipation in Uruguayan
society, to eliminate age-old prejudices and oppose the
ideological force of a bourgeoisie which defines the norms
of 'femininity', can only be conducted under conditions of
basic social, economic and cultural justice. Under present
conditions, women in Uruguay cannot restrict themselves
to pressing solely feminist demands. They cannot stay on
the sidelines of the social and ideological struggles being
fought in their country and in their continent, where even a
'neutral' position amounts to supporting the conservative
forces. Women can all too easily be tricked by the cultural

models of the dominant class and by attractive reforms which remain rooted in the perspective of that class. We only have to look at the way middle-class women with recently secured greater spending power can be diverted into satisfying the artificial needs produced by a society geared to conspicuous consumption.

The quest for formal equality with men isolates the problem and cuts it off from its roots, leading to a reformism which strengthens the psychological conditioning of women according to the models of the local bourgeoisie. To struggle for exclusively feminist demands without taking the national context into account leads to isolation and ideological alienation based on acceptance of a stereotyped model of female behaviour, a model which suits the needs of a developed capitalist society and thus rejects the national cultural forms corresponding to Latin American reality. The resulting acculturation, escapism and ignorance of the historical process prevents women from acquiring the collective and historical consciousness which is essential if neo-colonial domination and imperialism are to be destroyed.

Notes

1. The International Commission of Jurists, the World Council of Churches, the I.L.O., Amnesty International, the International Federation of Human Rights, the International Union of Students, the Red Cross, the International Peace Council, the Russell Tribunal, the World Trade Union Federation, the International Organization of Journalists, the World Association of Doctors, the Methodist Union of Churches (New York), the International Federation of Teaching Unions, the 4th Inter-American Conference on Education, etc.
2. C. Martinez Moreno, 'URUGUAY HOY—Crepusculo in Arcadia', Mexico: Siglo XXI.
3. *Latifundium*—big landholding geared to extensive farming.
4. The International Democratic Federation of Women expressed its concern at the wave of terror and violence in Uruguay and at the violation of human rights. In the name of 112 national women's organizations, in January 1976 the Federation called on the U.N. Commission on Human Rights to demand that the Uruguayan Government free its political prisoners, many of whom are women.

5. U.I.E., p. 24, sworn statement: 'I swear on my honour that I unconditionally and unreservedly support the democratic republican system of government adopted by the sovereign will of the Nation. I declare that I am not and have never been a member of one of the anti-national organizations dissolved by the Executive Authority, or of any other which seeks to undermine the present system of government. N.B. I accept that any deliberate falsification in the present declaration is an offence under Law No. 14248 of 1 August 1974 and under Article 239 of the Penal Code.'

6. Methodical torture has now been systematized, with the following as the most commonly used methods: (1) *The 'Stake'*: The prisoners are hooded and kept standing, without food or water, for hours or even days until they black out. As part of the process, they are made to excrete in their clothes. When they fall, they are dragged along by the hair, kicked until they stand again or doused with freezing water. Occasionally they are kept in this position out of doors, exposed to the elements in sub-zero weather. The treatment usually leads to inflammation of the legs, fainting and acute delirium; (2) *Blows* of every kind are regularly administered to the bound and hooded prisoners, using karate chops, wooden clubs, iron bars and rubber truncheons. Another method is the 'telephone', which consists in striking both the prisoner's ears simultaneously with the palms of the hand; (3) *Electrification*: The prisoners are hooded, bound naked to wooden or metal racks and drenched with water to ensure better conductivity. Electric current, sometimes up to 200 volts (220 volts is lethal) is then applied to the most sensitive parts of their bodies: the inside of their noses, their gums, lips, eyes, ears and genitals, frequently resulting in severe burns and heart attacks; (4) *The 'Submarine'*: The prisoners are bound to planks and submerged in tanks of water until they begin to drown. When the prisoners swallow too much water, a military doctor is called to revive them and the treatment goes on. The water in the tanks is invariably full of prisoners' vomit, blood and urine. Brief periods of interruption occur when the prisoners are placed within scorching distance of a fire in order to keep them responsive. Heart attacks are common. One variant is the 'Portuguese Submarine', in which the water is electrified while the victim is held under; (5) *The 'Dry Submarine'*: Polythene bags are put over the prisoners heads and tied round their necks, so that they suffocate. Nybia Sabalsagary died under this form of torture on 29 June 1974; (6) *The 'Horse'*: Naked prisoners are sat astride a crossbar so that their feet do not touch the ground. Their arms and legs are spreadeagled, then the crossbar is shaken for hours leaving the contact area torn and bleeding, and a general feeling of being sawn in two; (7) *Hangings*: Prisoners are hung up by

the wrists with metal wire, sometimes for days; (8) *'Pau de Arara'*: The prisoners are hung up by the knees over a bar, with their hands and feet bound together. The resulting restriction on blood circulation means that the body takes on a violet tinge and the prisoner eventually passes out; (9) *'Mock Execution'*: The prisoner is put through the elaborate rigmarole of being brought before a firing squad, then returned to the cell; (10) *Rape*: Both men and women are raped by their torturers and by trained dogs. Sticks and fists are forced up the vagina or the anus, producing severe wounds; (11) *The Grill*: The prisoners are bound to a coal-fired grill and released only when their torturers smell burning flesh.

Venezuela: Maternity Care and Class Discrimination

Working Class Women and the Health Service

What are the real problems posed by pregnancy? The question cannot be avoided: the changes which it operates in a woman's body are crucial, even if they are experienced differently according to the economic, social and cultural conditions which prevail in particular women's lives.

Progress has been made, both on the technical level (the pill, the coil, etc.) and in terms of social and cultural policies geared to make the process of maternity into a humanized and conscious choice. Nonetheless, Latin American women, especially those from the poorer sectors of society, still suffer from the indifference and irresponsibility of government maternity policies. The authorities have shown that they are quite willing to allow arbitrary and odious methods, such as sterilization, to be imposed from abroad, yet they seem quite incapable of providing their populations with any real information about contraception. This critique also applies to the medical staff, who themselves bear much of the responsibility for these problems; the class position of doctors is an integral aspect of the situation.

Reports from the wards of *Concepcion Palacios* Maternity Centre in Caracas show quite clearly that, the poorer a woman is, the more inhumanly she will be treated by the medical profession. 'The humanization of pregnancy is thus not just a question of changing the psychological and physiological context but also of instilling a new humanism in medical staff, without whom it cannot be achieved.'[1]

The *Concepcion Palacios* Maternity Centre in Caracas was set up to provide a service for poorer women, and is practically the only institution of its kind in the city and the surrounding area. Even some well-to-do women with special clinical problems use the Centre, for the simple reason that it is the best-equipped in the country. The 'Urgent Cases' Surgery Department is always full of women who are about to give birth or who are suffering from complications due to infection or the after-effects of botched abortions. If birth is imminent, the woman is hospitalized immediately, but if it is not, she is told to come back when she is just about to go into labour—the Centre's facilities are inadequate to cope with the number of women who attend. Preventive hospitalization is impossible, and all too often, even amongst those admitted, two women who have just given birth have to share the same bed.

When I visited the Centre, most of the women in the waiting room had come from the *cerros*, the poor districts built on the slopes of the hills around the city. Two of them had come from further out. One woman had had to leave home at five in the morning and had travelled for four hours. When I asked her if there were no maternity centres closer to her village, she told me that there was one but that she had had to come to Caracas because she wanted to have her fallopian tubes tied. The other woman who had also travelled a long distance had come for the same reason. She had arrived the previous day, but the doctors had told her to go home (she lives in Guarenus, about 100 kilometres from Caracas) and come back when she was about to give birth. This was despite the fact that this woman had already had six children and knew, on the basis of experience, that her seventh was imminent.

'I don't know what to do. I've no more money, and just imagine what it would be like if I set off and it happened on the journey.' This seemed fair comment. Travelling for four hours in a bus over a dangerous and bumpy road did not seem particularly advisable for a woman about to go into labour. The alternative was not attractive either: all she could do was remain in the waiting room, stuck in a chair. On top of which she had not eaten since the previous night. Every time the nurse came out to call for the next patient, she would turn to this poor woman and say, 'What are you still doing here, love, didn't they tell you to go away and come back later?'

One of the other women, who was expecting her ninth child, came from one of the shanty towns of Caracas. I asked her if she was also thinking of having her fallopian tubes tied. She answered with a timid gesture, indicating that she knew nothing about the subject. I tried to convince her to ask the doctor for information, at which point another woman intervened, saying, 'That's all very well, but you have to get your husband's consent for the operation.' Then someone else added that she 'knew somebody who had come to threaten the doctor for having tied his wife's fallopian tubes without his permission.'

'As if they were the ones who were going to look after the kids,' chipped in another women, 'they just pack their bags and go, without a thought for the children.'

Everybody began to join in the conversation. People started talking about looking after children and housework, about the many daily problems they had to cope with, the cost of living, unemployment and the difficulty of finding somewhere to leave the children while they were out at work. One of the main problems which emerged was finding someone to look after the children while the mothers were in hospital. Some of the women were more relaxed about this because they had grown-up daughters who could look after the domestic chores, care for the younger children, do the cooking and serve their father when he came in, etc.

'I've got four boys and now I'm hoping for a girl,' said somebody. A very young girl, who had arrived with a haemorrhage, said that she had worked for a wealthy family, and had been amazed to find that the daughter had got married without knowing anything at all about housework, expecting her Spanish husband to pay for a servant. 'But he refused to hire one. Quite right too. A woman who gets married ought to know all about housework and herself should look after her husband.'

I asked them if they thought that husbands should also do some of the housework. Some answered that it was perfectly normal for the woman to do it, since the husband went out to work and earned the money.

'Ah, but it isn't always like that', one of them

interrupted, 'I also work, and when I come home exhausted, it's always me who has to do all the housework.'

'Yes, men always expect women to do everything.'

'Don't you think the problem can be sorted out?' I asked, 'After all, if little boys were taught to help, to do the dishes, make the beds, etc., things would be a lot easier.'

Everybody agreed, but 'Well . . . boys, you know, they're much more disobedient.' And one of them added: 'I really hope that things change by the time my girls grow up, so that they can find a man who'll help them bring up the kids. As for us, let's face it, we've had it.'

Faced with all this misery, the big mural on the waiting room wall seemed almost grotesque, a reminder of the pitiful inadequacy of the government's policy on maternity.

Build Consciousness

We believe that this report shows how wrong certain groups are to underestimate people's potential, to treat them as irremediably passive creatures to whom the truth must be carried by activists. On the contrary, the latent consciousness and hidden strength of all these women stem directly from the truth they experience every day and from the oppression they encounter in all their relations with men, be they fathers, husbands, lovers or bosses. This consciousness is reinforced by the increasing material difficulties women encounter in their efforts to accomplish the very tasks the system sets them.

We believe that what needs to be done is to promote the circumstances which make consciousness possible, namely contact and dialogue amongst poor women themselves, a dialogue from which we must always be prepared to learn.

Notes

1. Claude Revault d'Allones, *Le mal joli*, Paris: editions 10/18, 1976, pp. 261–2.

Appendix 1: Basic Data

Country[1]	Area	Population			Population Density (per sq.km.)	Economically Active Population[2]				Per Capita G.N.P. (francs)
	Total	*Total*	*Men*	*Women*		*Total*	*%*	*%M*	*%F*	
Guadeloupe	1,779	312,724	153,462	159,262	196	89,980	28.8	38.5	19.5	6,300
Martinique	1,102	320,030	155,212	164,818	325	89,464	28.0	36.0	20.4	7,300
Bolivia	1,098,581	2,704,165	1,326,099	1,098,581	5	—	—	—	—	1,800
Colombia	1,138,914	24,772,508	12,138,429	12,633,979	21	8,257,502	29.8	47.6	11.9	2,760
Chile	756,945	8,834,820	4,311,600	4,523,220	14	2,607,360	29.5	46.4	13.3	3,500
Cuba	114,524	8,569,121	4,392,970	4,176,151	79	2,633,309	30.7	49.0	11.6	3,300
Ecuador	283,561	6,500,845	3,253,764	3,247,081	25	1,442,591	32.2	54.0	10.5	2,500
Mexico	1,972,547	48,225,238	24,065,614	24,159,624	29	12,909,540	26.8	42.6	10.2	5,600
Puerto Rico	8,897	2,712,033	1,329,949	1,382,084	347	683,790	25.2	35.4	15.4	12,300
Uruguay	177,508	2,763,964	1,355,854	1,408,110	17	1,012,271	39.0	58.9	19.3	5,300
Venezuela	912,050	10,721,522	5,349,711	5,371,811	13	3,014,674	28.1	43.7	12.6	10,500
El Salvador	21,393	3,549,260	1,760,618	1,788,642	166	1,314,857	37.0	78.5	21.5	2,000

Source: *U.N. Statistical Yearbook*, New York: 1971.

1. Latest available figures. For comparison: France has 96 inhabitants per sq.km. and a *per capita* G.N.P. of 27,000 francs.
2. As a percentage of total population.
3. Source: *Atlaseco.*, 1976.

Appendix 2: Women's Suffrage in Latin America

Country	Year of Introduction
U.S.	1920
Ecuador	1929
Puerto Rico	1929
Brazil	1932
Uruguay	1932
Cuba	1934
El Salvador	1939
Dominican Republic	1942
Guatemala	1945
Panama	1945
Venezuela	1946
Argentina	1947
Chile	1949
Costa Rica	1949
Martinique and Guadeloupe	1949
Haiti	1950
Bolivia	1952
Mexico	1953
Honduras	1955
Nicaragua	1955
Peru	1955
Colombia	1957
Paraguay	1961

Appendix 3: Unemployment and Working Women in Latin America

In Latin America, about 40 per cent of the active labour force is engaged in agriculture, an average figure which encompasses wide variations between countries, from El Salvador (60 per cent) to Uruguay (20 per cent). Low agricultural productivity in those regions where pre-capitalist relations of production still prevail, the expulsion of agricultural labourers as machines are introduced together with the high rate of population growth all combine to produce an exodus from the land. Yet in the industrial centres, despite expansion of the manufacturing sector, unemployment is increasing, particularly as the often spectacular growth of industry is for the most part linked to capital-intensive sectors. The economic dependence of the Latin American countries forces them to use techniques which rely on machines manufactured in the developed world, machines which have been designed to meet the needs of advanced industrial economies. However, the situation faced by such countries, where 1975 rates of growth were 3 per cent for unemployment, 2.6 per cent for the economy and 2.8 per cent for the population,[1] never features as a consideration in the purchase of this equipment.

Overall, the experience of capitalist growth in post-war Latin America is marked by the inability of the productive sectors to absorb the surplus rural and urban work force. Against this, there has been a steady increase in the size of the tertiary sector: from 1950 to 1970 the service and tertiary sector grew by 34.4 per cent whilst the industrial sector grew by only 6 per cent. Although the agricultural labour force actually grew by 75.5 per cent over the same period, the proportion of the total economically active population this represented fell by 22 per cent.[2]

One indication of the problem—which affects women more than men—is the fact that in 1960 some 40 per cent of the Latin American work force were underemployed and a further 27.4 per cent actually unemployed. Several studies into the causes of and possible remedies for this situation have been conducted, notably the 1969 CEPAL investigation which recommended various measures by which the G.N.P. could be made to grow at a rate sufficient to eliminate unemployment by 1980. The striking thing about these calculations was that they were based on the presupposition that *women's level of participation in the economically active population would remain static.*[3] In effect, the problem of employment has largely been neglected in Latin American 'planning and development programmes'. Employment has 'in most cases been treated as a side-effect of plans formulated in terms of other overall goals, for example growth rates, foreign trade and investment.'[4] Since employment in general has been considered as an effect rather than as a variable to be influenced in the different plans and programmes aimed at boosting the Latin American economies, it is hardly surprising that it was assumed that women's employment would remain static. It is only very recently that the importance of women's role in the economically active population has been recognized or that the possibility of changing this role has been seen as something 'which may become a goal for development policy, given its present low level and the potential reservoir of human resources it represents.'[5]

Much work still needs to be done before a realistic model of women's employment in Latin America can be constructed. But, since the concept of women's work remains vague and since the various specialized reports and economic investigations provide no precise figures, we can only offer a very general schema. Specific studies will have to take the conditions particular to each country into account. Nonetheless, the position of the active female work force in the various Latin American countries does exhibit certain common features (see Table 1).

Table 1
Economically Active Population in Latin America[1]

Country	Economically Active Population[2] (million)		Economically Active Women as a % of Total Population	Economically Active Women as a % of Female Population
	Total	Women		
Argentina	9.0	2.3	25.4	19.4
Brazil	37.8	11.7	30.9	23.6
Colombia	6.0	1.6	26.2	15.4
Costa Rica	0.6	0.1	19.3	12.1
Cuba[3]	2.6	0.5	18.3	11.5
Chile	2.6	0.6	23.1	13.3
Dominican Republic	1.2	0.3	25.7	15.9
Ecuador	1.9	0.3	16.9	9.8
El Salvador	1.3	0.4	29.3	21.5
Guadeloupe	0.1	0.05	43.9	—
Guatemala	1.5	0.2	14.0	8.4
Haiti	2.3	1.1	47.3	49.1
Jamaica	1.0	0.4	46.0	37.9
Martinique	0.1	0.04	39.4	22.9
Mexico	16.6	3.6	21.6	12.0
Nicaragua	0.5	0.1	21.9	11.5
Panama	0.5	0.1	25.6	17.8
Paraguay	0.8	0.1	21.4	13.6
Peru	3.9	0.8	20.7	11.8
Puerto Rico	0.9	0.3	31.3	17.4
Uruguay	1.0	0.3	24.9	19.3
Venezuela	3.7	1.0	27.8	17.3

Source: Drawn from I.L.O. figures, I.L.O., Geneva, 1975 and 1976.
1. Latest available figures.
2. The methods used to calculate the economically active population vary. They include totals from census forms, samples from census results, sample surveys, evaluations based on growth-rate projections, etc. There is also no uniform definition of age groups or conceptualization of unemployment, nor has it been possible to obtain figures relating to the same year. However, the table above does provide a rough guide to women's level of participation in the economically active population.
3. Excluding domestic staff.

Table 1 provides some basis for explaining Latin American women's massive and forced entry into the service sector, especially domestic service. The economic structure of these countries is incapable of absorbing the entire female work force, and the rate of unemployment amongst women is particularly high.[6] In 1960, 57.5 per cent of women employees were working in the service sectors and it is generally true that 2 out of 5 working women work as servants (see Table 2). In the countries where industry is weak and the tertiary sector small, agriculture still accounts for a high proportion of working women, as in Haiti, Paraguay, Guatemala and Honduras, amongst others.

Table 2
Female Employment in the Service Sector in 4 Latin American Countries, 1960 (%)

	Brazil		Chile		Colombia		Peru	
	A	B	A	B	A	B	A	B
Total for all services	100	69	100	62	100	62	100	1
Administration[1]	4	3	3	14	4	3	4	2
Social Services[2]	22	15	22	9				
Public Administration	n.a.	n.a.	15	9	21	13	32	16
Domestic Services	54	37	58	36	73	45	60	31
Others	20	14	3	2	2	1	4	2

A=Percentage of women employed in service sector as a whole.
B=Percentage of total urban female economically active population. Drawn from PREALC, *La mujer y el empleo in America latina*, Geneva: I.L.O., 1976.
Source: Drawn from J.C. Elizaga, 'The Participation of Women in the Labour Force of Latin America, Fertility and Other Factors', *Women Workers*, Geneva: I.L.O., 1976.
1. Includes Army and police.
2. Includes education, health and social security.

In the countries where women have gone into industry to a great extent, this has not necessarily meant that their standard of living has gone up. They mainly occupy administrative positions and get lower wages than men (see Table 3). Often the work they are forced to do involves a higher level of exploitation.[7] In many cases technological advances have displaced women workers in industry, as is clear from examples in Venezuela, Brazil, Chile and Peru.[8] When the new machines come in, it is the women, even more than the men, who tend to lose their jobs. Sexual discrimination at work is also on the increase generally, notably in terms of access, promotion, salaries and 'perks'.[9] For example, a study of one particular category of jobs in Venezuela showed that the men's salaries were 60 per cent higher than the women's. Also in Venezuela, there are indications that the division of labour according to sex is becoming more pronounced,[10] while in Mexico the disparities in salary and 'perks' are quite blatant. In Puerto Rico industrial modernization has displaced many women, most of whom find it very difficult to secure a new job.

Slaves of Slaves

Table 3
Distribution of Income according to Sex in 3 Latin American
Countries (%)

Country, Year and Income Level[1]	Total	Men	Women
Colombia, all employees, 1970			
Low income	40	38	47
Middle income	59	61	53
High income	1	1	0
Chile, non-agricultural workers, 1968			
Low income	14	7	27
Middle income	83	89	72
High income	3	4	1
Chile, non-agricultural employees and entrepreneurs, 1968			
Low income	22	15	38
Middle income	71	75	60
High income	7	10	2
Panama, non-agricultural employees, 1972			
Low income	17	6	34
Middle income	77	85	64
High income	6	9	2

Source: Drawn from national surveys of households carried out by CEPAL-BIRF in H. Kirsch, 'La participacion de la mujer en los mercados de trabajo en latino-america', *Notas de Poblacion*, Ano III, Vol. 7, Santiago de Chile, 1975, p. 27.
1. The categorizations used for income groups in the various countries are not strictly equivalent. Our category 'low income' embraces the various bottom categories in the respective national classifications, 'high income' embraces the two top categories, and 'middle income' covers all the intermediate groupings. Drawn from PREALC (Programa regional del empleo pora America latina y al Caraibe) *La mujer y el empleo in America latina*, BIT, Geneva, 1976.

The idea that increased industrialization necessarily results in greater participation in the economically active population by women is clearly erroneous. One need only turn back to Table 1 to see that in Martinique and El Salvador, two of the least industrialized countries, 40 per cent and 30 per cent of their respective economically active populations are women. Working women are benefiting less and less from capitalist industrialization, and some authors even argue that their economic situation is actually getting worse.[11] In any case, industrialization, the growth of the tertiary sector, urbanization and even capitalist development itself have weakened Latin American women's position in the labour market. Their role as a reserve labour force has been accentuated. Women's power and representation in society have thus remained very restricted.

Table 4
Proportion of Women in the Economically Active Population by Age Group (%)

Country	Year	Age Group 15–24	25–44	45–54	55+	Overall Proportion[1]
Argentina	1960	37	25	18	8	24
	1970	37	31	24	9	27
Brazil[2]	1950	22	14	12	10	16
	1970	26	20	18	10	20
Colombia	1964	24	20	19	12	20
	1973	28	24	19	10	24
Chile	1960	29	24	20	12	23
	1970	23	21	20	10	21
Mexico	1960	16	15	19	20	17
	1970	22	16	16	13	18
Panama	1960	27	23	27	14	25
	1970	34	32	27	23	32
Peru[3]	1961	28	21	21	13	22
	1972	21	22	19	12	20

Source: Drawn from PREALC population censuses.
1. Corresponds to percentage of women in total economically active population. The variations from Table 1 are due either to the fact that the first age group has not been included (e.g. 12–14 in Mexico) or perhaps to the figures having been drawn from preliminary versions of the various censuses.
2. Different age group categories: 15–24, 25–39, 40–49 and 50+.
3. Different age groups categories: 15–24, 25–29, 30–49 and 50+.

Table 5
Education Level of Active Population in 5 Latin American Countries (1960 & 1970) by Sex (%)

| | Completed Years of Study | | | | | |
| | 1960 | | | 1970 | | |
Country	None	1–5	6 or more	None	1–5	6 or more
Argentina						
Men	8	75	17	0	42	58
Women	6	68	26	0	32	68
Brazil						
Men	42	51	7	No Data Available		
Women	42	46	12			
Chile						
Men	16	59	25	11	56	33
Women	12	58	26	6	49	45
Mexico						
Men	36	57	7	28	60	12
Women	31	52	17	26	59	15
Panama						
Men	25	57	18	20	58	22
Women	9	53	38	9	50	41

Source: Drawn from CEPAL/UNICEF, 'Programma de analisis de censos para los censos de 1970' in H. Kirsch, 'La participacion de la mujer en los mercados de trabajo en latino-america', *Notas de Poblacion*, Ano III, Vol. 7, Santiago de Chile, 1975.

The effects of all this can be seen in Tables 4 and 5, where sexual discrimination emerges as an especially striking feature. The situation is not very surprising since 'women, like certain ethnic groups, are treated as pariahs. Pariahs, as a whole, form a secondary stratum within the working class, and this secondary stratum plays an important role within the overall system. Since they are particularly badly paid, the women are used as a means to bring down average salaries and as a threat to the rest of the working class, who fear that they themselves may be replaced or forced to accept a lower salary. Discrimination against women thus contributes to a general lowering of working-class salaries.'[12]

Leaving aside the general economic and social characteristics of underdeveloped countries and their impact on employment, there are specific differences between the countries concerned which must be taken into account. For instance, the rate of population growth is a decisive long-term factor affecting the demand for labour. In countries where this rate is very high, unemployment hits all workers, but women especially. Apart from in the domestic service sector, men will find it much easier than women to get jobs when demand is low. In the more industrialized countries such as Brazil, Mexico and Venezuela, the proportion of women in the economically active population is substantially higher. In Haiti and Guadeloupe, where the rate reaches 50 per cent, emigration is a crucial feature. On the other hand, in Mexico, despite a high level of emigration, the annual population growth rate over the last thirty years has been over 3 per cent.

Clearly the growth of the population is not a problem in itself. Like many other factors, it only becomes so when it is accompanied by an economic structure which cannot provide productive employment for the whole population. The main obstacle to a resolution of employment and population 'problems' in Latin America is precisely the present economic structure.

Finally, a word of warning. Given that the present methods and norms used in census work are incapable of detecting the full range of women's activities, the tables presented in this appendix should be treated with a certain reserve. The estimates and projections as to the composition of the labour force elaborated by the I.L.O. and other sources should be treated with caution. Differences from one country to another are difficult to explain and the concept of women's work seems to be very different from the concept of work used in the census and labour statistics. For country by country figures, see Table 1.[13]

Table 6
Economically Active Women as a Percentage of Total Female Population, 1965–1985

	1965	1975	1985
World	29.16	27.88	26.62
U.S.	25.50	27.89	28.86
Canada	20.93	24.79	27.29
Latin America	12.38	12.01	11.76
Tropical Latin America[1]	11.45	11.19	10.99
Central America[2]	9.23	9.10	9.10
Temperate Latin America[3]	15.65	15.37	15.30
Caribbean[4]	20.26	19.97	20.10

Source: I.L.O., 'Proyecciones de la fuerza de trabajo, 1965–1985', *Tasas de actividad femenina, 1965–1985*, Geneva, 1971, Table 5.
1.   Tropical Latin America: Bolivia, Brazil, Colombia, Ecuador, Guyana, Peru, Venezuela.
2.   Central America: Mexico, Guatemala, El Salvador, Honduras, Nicaragua, Costa Rica, Panama et al.
3.   Temperate Latin America: Argentina, Chile, Uruguay, Paraguay.
4.   Caribbean: Cuba, Haiti, Dominican Republic, Puerto Rico, Jamaica, Trinidad and Tobago, Barbados, et al.

Notes

1. UNO-CEPAL, *Estudio economico para America latina*, New York, 1975, Vol. 1, pp. 41–2.
2. Juan Milos and Eduardo Morgan, *Factores economicos que influyen en la politica de trabajo y poblacion en America latina*, Geneva: I.I.E.L., 1974, p. 23.
3. UNO-CEPAL, *El segundo decenio de las Naciones Unidas para el desarrollo—Los deficits virtuales de commercio y de ahorro interno y la desocupacion estructural de America latina*, Lima: 1969, p. 85.
4. Milos and Morgan, *op. cit.,* p. 94.
5. *Ibid.,* p. 95.
6. Cf. I.L.O.—P.R.E.A.L.C. Report, Part II, 'Condiciones de trabajo y el empleo de la mujer', Geneva: 1976, p. 25.
7. Mercedes Olivera, 'La opresion de la mujer en el sistema capitalista', *Historia y Sociedad*, No. 6, Segunda epoca, Mexico: 1975, p. 5. See also Isabel Larguia and John Dumoulin, 'Aspectos de la condicion laboral de la mujer', *Revista Casa de las Americas*, No. 88, Havana: 1975, pp. 45–70.
8. Elsa Chaney and Marianne Schmink, 'Las mujeres y la modernisacion, acceso a la tecnologia', *La mujer en America latina*, Mexico: Sepsetentas, 1975, Vol. 1, p. 15.
9. I.L.O., *op. cit.,* p. 28.
10. *Ibid.,* p. 29 and Marianne Schmink, *Dependent Development and the Division of Labour by Sexes*, San Francisco: 1974, p. 15.
11. Chaney and Schmink, *op. cit.,* pp. 25 and 47. See also I.L.O., *op. cit.,* p. 29.
12. Jurgen Kuczynski, quoted by Larguia and Dumoulin, *op. cit.,* p. 55.
13. See P.R.E.A.L.C., *La mujer y el empleo en America latina*, Geneva: I.L.O., 1976.